Energy, Economics, and the Environment

Case Studies and Teaching Activities
for High School

Indiana Department of Education
Center for School Improvement and Performance

Originally published 1994

Revised 2006

Acknowledgements - Original Edition

Curriculum Designers/Authors

Harlan Day, Economics Education Consultant
Indiana Department of Education

Deborah Christopher, Teacher
Delaware Community Schools

Kate Ferguson, Teacher (retired)
Fort Wayne Community School Corporation

Pam George, Teacher
Northwest Allen County Schools

Corporate Sponsors

Indiana Michigan Power

Indianapolis Power and Light Company

Northern Indiana Public Service Company

PSI Energy

Curriculum Committee

Marty Alenduff
Indiana Department of Education

David Ballard
Indiana Department of Education

Mike Brian
Indiana Michigan Power

Sam Carman
Indiana Department of Natural Resources

Brian Cohee
Indiana Department of Environmental Management

Bob Golobish
Indianapolis Power and Light Company

Peter Harrington
Indiana Council for Economic Education

Dennis Harris
Indiana Department of Commerce

Robert Harris
Economics Department, IUPUI

Betty Johnson
Indiana Department of Education

Kate Ferguson
Environmental Education Coalition

Julie Houston
Northern Indiana Public Service Company

Jeanna Keller
PSI Energy

Jackie Williams
Northern Indiana Public Service Company

Paul Torcellini
Project NEED

Edward Wills, Jr.
Indianapolis Power and Light Company

Joe Wright
Indiana Department of Education

Supporting Agencies

Environmental Education Coalition

Indiana Council for Economic Education

Indiana Department of Commerce

Indiana Department of Education

Indiana Department of Environmental Management

Indiana Department of Natural Resources

Indiana Michigan Power

Indiana NEED Project

Indiana Petroleum Council

Indianapolis Power and Light Company

IUPUI Center for Economic Education

Northern Indiana Public Service Company

PSI Energy

Special Recognition

Center for School Improvement and Performance, Indiana Department of Education,
for coordinating and supervising the development of the EEE curriculum
(Special thanks to Christy Skinner for preparing the many drafts and final draft)

Rosanne Russell, Division of Publications, Indiana Department of Education,
for preparing the camera-ready final draft

PSI Energy, for preparing the front cover

Linda Lentz, teacher at Indianapolis Public School #68, and her students,
for field-testing activities in the EEE curriculum

PSI Energy, Indiana Michigan Power, and Northern Indiana Public Service Company,
for printing the EEE curriculum

Commitment to EEE Program

The EEE program will be promoted through workshops, institutes, and conferences
for teachers. We welcome new EEE members who believe in the philosophy and
goals of the EEE curriculum. For further information, contact the
Indiana Department of Education (800-527-4930)
or the Indiana Council for Economic Education (765-494-8545).

Acknowledgements – 2006 Revision

Content review of *Energy, Economics, and the Environment (EEE)* was provided by **Mike Ellerbrock,** Ph.D., Director of the Virginia Tech Center for Economic Education. Dr. Ellerbrock was the 2002 recipient of USDA's National Award for Teaching Excellence in Agriculture, Natural Resources, Human and Veterinary Sciences and is a member of the Governor's Commission on Environmental Education in Virginia.

Sincere thanks are due to **Indiana Michigan Power** for its ongoing financial support over the years for teacher training programs that support the *Energy, Economics, and the Environment* curriculum. Indiana Michigan Power's dedication to economics education is exemplary.

Shelly Surber, Indiana Council for Economic Education, and Purdue student, **Patti Aquino**, contributed significantly to the final formatting of this revised publication.

Funding for this revision of *Energy, Economics, and the Environment* was provided by the **National Council on Economic Education (NCEE)**. *Energy, Economics, and the Environment* is distributed exclusively by the NCEE.

National Council on Economic Education
1140 Avenue of the Americas
New York, NY 10036
Phone: 212.730.7007 or 1.800.338.1192
www.ncee.net
Email: sales@ncee.net

Table of Contents

Correlation of Energy, Economics, and the Environment with the National Standards for Economics*

Standards ↓ Lessons ➡	Introductory Essay	1	2	3	4
1. Scarcity	√	√	√	√	√
• Goods & Services	√				
• Producers	√		√	√	
• Consumers	√				
• Productive Resources	√		√		
• Opportunity Cost	√	√	√	√	√
2. Marginal costs/marginal benefits	√	√	√	√	√
3. Allocation of goods and services	√	√	√		
4. Role of incentives	√	√	√	√	√
5. Gain from trade					
6. Specialization and trade					
7. Markets: price and quantity determination			√		
8. Role of price in market system		√	√	√	
9. Role of competition					
10. Role of economic institutions (especially property rights)	√	√	√	√	√
11. Role of money					
12. Role of interest rates					
13. Role of resources in determining income					
14. Profit and the entrepreneur			√	√	
15. Growth	√			√	√
16. Role of government	√	√	√	√	√
17. Using cost/benefit analysis to evaluate government programs	√	√	√	√	√
18. Macroeconomy-income/employment, prices					
19. Unemployment and inflation				√	
20. Monetary and fiscal policy					

* *Voluntary National Content Standards in Economics,* copyright © 1997, National Council on Economic Education

Rationale

One of the great challenges facing educators is to teach students how to be responsible stewards of the natural resources entrusted to them. This is especially true today since our growing worldwide population inevitably exerts greater strains on our environment and on our fiscal and natural resources. As individuals and as a society, we must be prepared to deal with the problems that will challenge us in the decades ahead. The purpose of the *Energy, Economics, and the Environment* (EEE) curriculum is to provide students with the necessary knowledge and skills to help solve these problems.

The curriculum focuses on three important subjects: energy, economics, and the environment. One of the key assumptions of this booklet is the interrelatedness of these three areas of study. It is virtually impossible to study one of these subjects without encountering the others. Indeed, the failure to consider the interdependence of environmental, energy, and economic issues will result in flawed policy decisions that will diminish the potential for maintaining a strong economic system, a healthy environment, and a sustainable energy resource base.

In order to deal with these complex issues, students must be trained in three important areas. First, they must be taught basic knowledge and concepts about energy, the environment, and economics as well as the fundamental interrelationships of all three. Second, they must learn effective decision-making skills. Third, they must be involved in meaningful, motivating learning activities. As a result of participating in the EEE program, students will understand the trade-offs that are involved in ensuring a quality environment, the wise use of energy resources, and a vibrant economy. Thus, our students will be better equipped to meet the environmental and energy challenges of the future.

Overview

Nearly every day in the news there are stories dealing with the economic implications of energy and environmental issues. How can high school students make sense of these complicated issues? What do they need to know in order to make wise decisions as consumers, producers, and voting citizens?

Purpose of the Energy, Economics, and Environment Curriculum

One purpose of this curriculum is to provide teachers and students with a conceptual framework for analyzing energy and environmental issues, especially in regards to economics. Teachers will notice that Part 1 of the Introduction to this booklet explains the basic economic concepts that provide the conceptual framework. Part 2 of the Introduction explains how to use a five-step, decision-making model to analyze energy and environmental issues.

A second purpose of this curriculum is to provide teachers with a set of four motivating, interdisciplinary teaching units. Each unit focuses on a particular energy and/or environmental theme and has three basic elements: 1. basic information, 2. a set of classroom teaching activities, and 3. a case study. In each case study, students use a five-step, decision-making model to investigate and solve an energy/environmental problem. Each unit includes basic facts and vocabulary about the issue being studied.

The classroom teaching activities require students to apply skills across several areas of the curriculum. Some activities also require students to make extensive use of resources in their communities. Each unit contains these special section titles: Debating the Issues, Further Investigations, and EEE Actions – You Can Make a Difference!

A Starting Point for Analysis

The issues covered in the four teaching units are water pollution, forest resources, renewable energy resources, and global warming. These are complex topics, and there is constantly new information available concerning them. You should therefore view this curriculum as a *starting point for analysis*. As you read articles or gather new information about these topics, add them to the curriculum. This will keep your *Energy, Economics, and the Environment* curriculum up to date.

Curriculum Organization

Introduction

Part 1:   **A Framework for Analysis**
- Fundamental Ideas and Relationships
- Three Important Economic Considerations

Part 2:   **A Decision-Making Model: A Tool for Analysis**

Teaching Units

All units contain three elements:

1. Basic Information
- Basic Facts About the Issue
- Vocabulary

2. Teacher Instructions
- Important Concepts to Emphasize
- Teaching Suggestions
- Key Questions to Ask Students

3. Classroom Teaching Activities
- Specific Activities
- Further Investigations
- Debating the Issues
- EEE Actions – You Can Make a Difference!
- Case Study
- Answers to Selected Teaching Activities

Introduction

Part 1: A Framework for Analysis

This section provides a general economic framework for analyzing environmental and energy issues. Without such a framework, any analysis of these critical issues will be deficient. Students (future policy makers) must understand the basic economic concepts that relate to these issues in order to make wise environmental and energy policy decisions.

Fundamental Ideas and Relationships

The Necessity of Production

In every society, people require **goods** and **services** that will enable them to survive and prosper. *A fundamental principle of economics is that these goods and services must be produced.* Without production of some sort, survival would be virtually impossible.

Fortunately, every society is endowed with resources which can be used to produce goods and services. These resources, called **productive resources (factors of production)**, can be classified into three groups: natural resources (land), labor (human) resources, and capital resources. **Natural resources**, both renewable and nonrenewable, come from nature. Examples include coal, water, trees, air, and the land itself. **Labor resources (human resources)** refer to the mental and physical work effort expended in production and to the entrepreneurial skills needed to guide production. **Capital resources** are physical goods used to produce other goods and services such as buildings, tools, equipment, and machinery. Figure 1 illustrates how productive resources are combined to produce goods and services.

The problem for individuals and society is that the desire for most goods and services is **unlimited**, whereas productive resources are **limited**. This tension between unlimited wants and the limited productive resources available for satisfying these wants is what economists refer to as **scarcity**. *Every society, rich or poor, confronts the basic economic problem of scarcity.* [1]

---

1. Note that a distinction exists between the economic notion of scarcity versus the physical concept. For example, economists would say that 4-leaf clovers are *not* scarce, even though there are few of them, if consumers do not desire them.

Figure 1

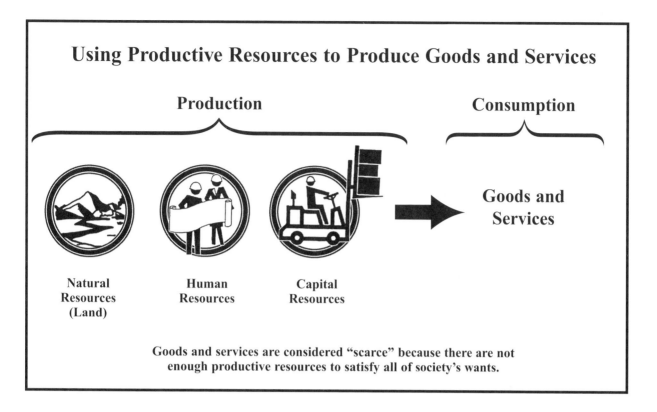

Using Productive Resources to Produce Goods and Services

Production   Consumption

Goods and Services

Natural Resources (Land)   Human Resources   Capital Resources

Goods and services are considered "scarce" because there are not enough productive resources to satisfy all of society's wants.

Production and Energy

So where does energy fit into our discussion? First, *energy is something that consumers desire.* All of us consume energy in one way or another - to heat our homes, cook our food, or power our cars.

Second, *energy is necessary for production.* Without some form of energy, the production of goods and services would virtually cease. Thus, energy is an integral component of both the production and consumption side of the diagram (Figure 2).

Third, *most forms of energy, like productive resources, are scarce.* With the exception of thermal energy from the sun, energy resources are not free goods, available in unlimited quantities at a zero price. Quite the contrary, energy sources, including the sun's thermal energy, are costly to harness, develop, and use. Because energy is scarce, its value is reflected in our market system by prices. *The price of an energy resource gives an indication of how scarce the resource is relative to other resources.*

Sometimes an energy shortage may occur, as in the 1970s, when there were long gas lines. A shortage is caused when a producer or government agency fixes the price of a good or service below its natural market level. Even when there is no energy shortage, energy is still a scarce resource. One must still pay to obtain it.

Figure 2

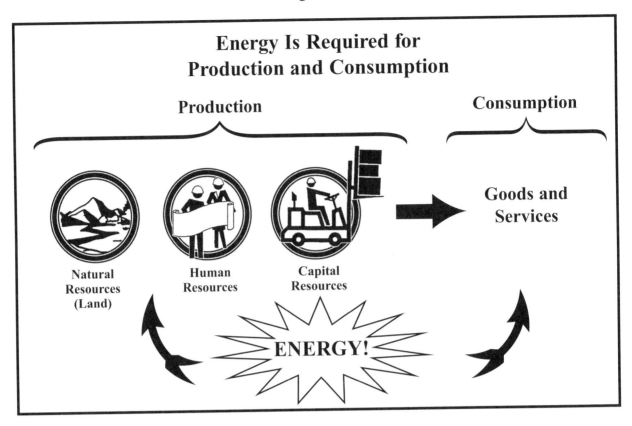

Production and the Environment

Now we can examine how the environment affects our simple model of production and energy use. *All production and consumption must take place within the context of the environment.* As such, the environment affects and is affected by production and consumption. This is evident when examining three basic services provided by the environment.

Services Provided by the Environment

First, the environment provides us with the **natural resources**, including energy resources, needed to produce goods and services. As we learned above, natural resources are one of the basic productive resources.

Second, the environment is a natural **"waste sink"** for the inevitable by-products/wastes of both production and consumption. In earlier times, organic wastes were more common and were more easily degraded by the environment. However, in modern times many wastes are not easily degraded and are present in larger quantities, resulting in more serious pollution problems for society.

Third, the environment provides us with many **"ecological services"** such as biodiversity, air and water filtration, soil fertility, carbon sequestration, sustainable populations of wildlife, rodent and disease control, scientific knowledge, medical research, pharmacological applications, and natural amenities, such as beautiful wilderness areas, scenic forests, and bodies of water for swimming, boating, and fishing.

Figure 3 expands our production diagram, illustrating the services provided by the environment.

Figure 3

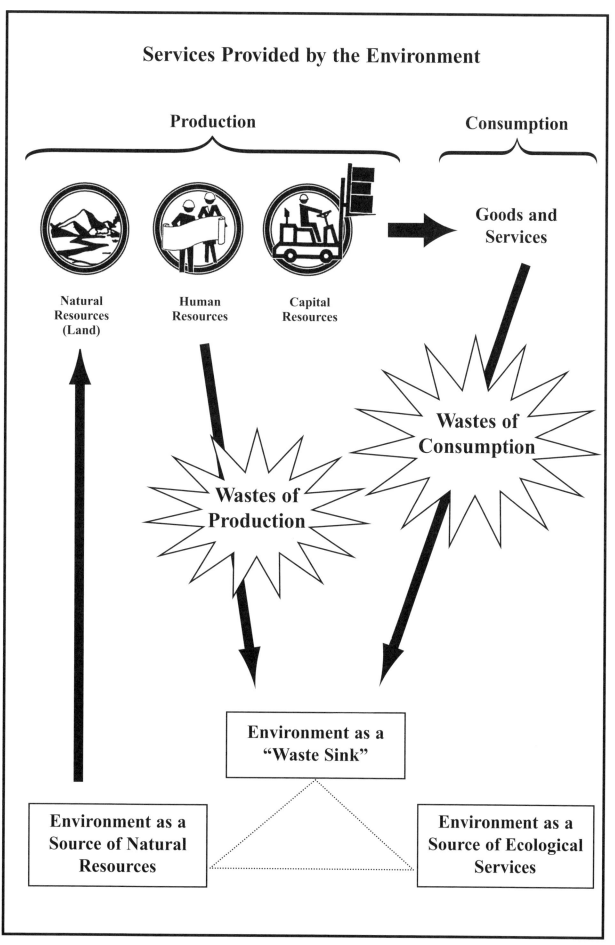

Services Provided by the Environment

Production

Consumption

Natural
Resources
(Land)

Human
Resources

Capital
Resources

Goods and
Services

Wastes of
Consumption

Wastes of
Production

Environment as a
"Waste Sink"

Environment as a
Source of Natural
Resources

Environment as a
Source of Ecological
Services

Summary

The four statements below summarize what we have discussed so far. They provide a starting point for analysis.

A Starting Point for Analysis

1. To survive and prosper, societies must produce goods and services. Every society has productive resources (natural resources, labor resources, and capital resources) that it uses to produce goods and services.

2. Energy is necessary in both production and consumption. Energy sources originate from natural resources. Because most forms of energy are scarce, both producers and consumers must pay to obtain energy.

3. The production and consumption of goods and services generates waste materials, which must be recycled or properly disposed.

4. Using the environment for production, consumption, and waste disposal affects the ecological and amenity services provided by the environment.

Three Important Economic Considerations

There are three critically important economic concepts to consider when analyzing environmental and energy issues: **opportunity cost/trade-offs, spillover costs** (negative externalities), and **marginalism**. They are discussed below.

1. Opportunity Cost and Trade-Offs

The basic economic problem of scarcity forces individuals and societies to choose how to use their limited productive resources. For example, money spent purchasing a bicycle cannot be spent on a new television. Tax monies spent on environmental protection and pollution control cannot be spent on national defense. Choices must be made.

Any time a choice is made among alternatives, there are specific alternatives that are *not* chosen. The value of the best alternative *not* chosen is called the **opportunity cost**. *Because productive resources are scarce, there is an opportunity cost to every economic decision.*

When a person or society decides to produce or consume one good instead of another, they are making a **trade-off** - they are trading off less of one thing for more of something else. For example, when a society decides to spend $5 million less on cancer research and instead decides to use the money to purchase land for a national park, the society is trading off better cancer treatment for its citizens for more environmental protection and recreation. It is hoped that the benefits from the park outweigh the potential benefits of the medical research.

The value of what is received when making a trade-off is an estimate of the benefit of the decision. The value of what is given up in making a trade-off is a measure of opportunity cost. The opportunity cost is sometimes measured in dollars, as noted above, where the opportunity cost of using $5 million to help purchase land for a national park is the lost benefits from $5 million *not* invested in cancer research.

Figure 4

Trade-Offs and Opportunity Cost

Cancer Research   **National Park**

$5 Million Dollars

Society is trading off cancer research for improved environmental protection and recreation. The opportunity cost of choosing a national park is the lost benefits of $5 million dollars spent on cancer research.

One major difficulty in analyzing environmental issues is that it is sometimes difficult to measure the monetary value of opportunity costs. What is the money value of clean air or a clean river? Not surprisingly, individuals differ greatly in this valuation. One person may easily endure moderate amounts of air pollution in a certain area, whereas another person may consider even the smallest amounts of pollution to be intolerable. Despite the difficulty, innovative techniques have been developed by economists to measure opportunity costs to help policy makers when analyzing energy and environmental issues. For example:

- *Contingent Valuation* – randomized surveys with hypothetical questions asking citizens how much money they would be willing to pay to protect a specific natural resource, or how much they would have to be compensated to accept losing a resource.

- *Hedonic Pricing* – inferring the value of a specific natural resource based on the changes in value of related goods (e.g., adjacent real estate) that possess some of the same characteristics or provide some of the same services.

- *Travel Cost Method* – inferring the value of a specific natural resource by extrapolating visitors' actual travel costs to include a hypothetical user fee paid by tourists/sportspersons from various distances to visit the site.

2. Spillover Costs

We have learned that the production and consumption of goods and services, including energy, will cause some waste to flow into the environment. This is unavoidable because societies must have goods and services in order to survive and prosper. Also, not all "waste" causes "pollution" because some waste is assimilable by the environment.

However, a major problem arises when the negative effects (costs) of waste flows are imposed on individuals, plants (flora), or animals (fauna) *not* involved in the buying and selling decisions that cause the flows. That is, there are serious problems when the costs of waste flows are imposed on "innocent bystanders" (or ecosystems) who are *external* to the production and consumption decisions that result in the waste flows. Economists refer to these imposed costs as **negative externalities,** or **spillover costs** (Figure 5). In modern times the problem of spillover costs is compounded by the increasing *volume* of waste, as well as by the changing *nature* of waste (less biodegradable, more toxic, etc.).

Air and water pollution is an example of a spillover cost, or negative externality. When a paper mill produces products, it ejects waste materials into the air and water. Individuals who breathe the air near the paper mill or who use the contaminated water bear the brunt of these external costs, even though these individuals may not benefit from the production or consumption of the paper products made in the mill. *An additional problem occurs if no one owns the air or water, and there is therefore no private cost for using these natural resources.* Because the use of the air and water is free, the mill actually has shifted some of the cost of paper production onto other individuals. The result is that too many paper products are produced, and their price is less than it would be if all the costs were taken into account. Also, nearby citizens suffer declining property values and diminished quality of life.

Figure 5

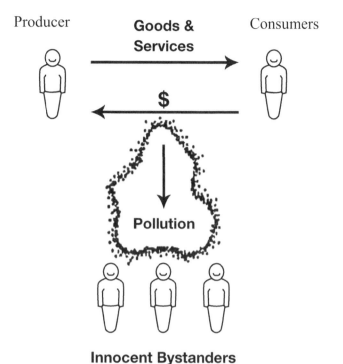

Pollution Hurts Innocent Bystanders

The producers and consumers both benefit from the production and consumption of goods and services. However, innocent bystanders sometimes receive the negative effects of the pollution created in production. This especially occurs when natural resources used in production, such as air and water, are commonly owned.

Dealing with Spillovers

What do societies do to correct the effects of negative spillover costs on the environment and on individuals? Some common courses of action are discussed below.

Rules and Regulations

The most typical way used to reduce spillover costs is through rules and regulations. A government agency (e.g. U.S. Environmental Protection Agency, state Department of Natural Resources) may impose regulations which define strict limits on waste discharge or may set certain standards for air pollution or waste disposal. Examples include the mandated emissions standards for automobiles or the required use of "coal scrubbers"

in plants where coal is the source of energy. Government may even ban a certain type of production all together, as in the case of oil drilling in certain wilderness areas.

Rules and regulations are popular since they seem to provide a simple and direct solution to spillover problems. However, regulations can be costly to implement and enforce. They tend to treat all (major and minor) violators the same, thus raising issues of fairness and efficiency. Regulations also limit individual freedom.

Taxing Production

Another method used by government (federal or state) is to tax the production activity that produced the spillover. Taxing a product increases its price, thereby reducing the quantity of the product that is produced and consumed. This results in fewer spillover costs, and also raises tax monies that can be used for improving the environment. An example of this method is the excise tax on gasoline, tires, and coal production.

Subsidies

A third method used by government is subsidies. A subsidy is the opposite of a tax. A government gives money (directly or in the form of tax breaks) to firms to encourage them to reduce spillovers. For example, monies given to a firm may be used to install modern equipment, help clean a river, or revitalize land marred by surface mining. Subsidies may be unpopular since taxpayers may not wish to use public monies to pay for spillovers caused by private firms, even though taxpayers will benefit generally from less pollution in their community.

Creating Proper Incentives

In recent years, new methods for reducing the harmful effects of negative externalities have been proposed. These methods provide more efficient solutions to spillover problems because they emphasize creating proper incentives for individual action. The goal is to make it more profitable (cost effective) to act in a socially responsible manner.

Impose Effluent or Emission Taxes

One way to create proper incentives is by imposing effluent or emission taxes. This approach imposes a fee on each unit of pollution discharged into the environment. This tax provides an incentive for firms to devise creative ways to reduce emissions and also provides tax monies for pollution management. Firms could still choose *not* to reduce emissions, but they would have to bear the cost of the decision. The external costs imposed on others would therefore be "internalized." Effluent and emission taxes can be a wise course of action because the tax is on the pollution *discharge*, not the production activity itself. This provides more of an incentive for economic growth and development.

Define Property Rights

Most economists believe that assigning and enforcing property rights more effectively will create incentives for more responsible social behavior. The logic goes like this: If property is commonly owned, like the air or waterways, it will be overused or abused. In contrast, if property is privately owned, the owner has a strong incentive to maintain or improve the value of the property. For example, a timber company has a financial incentive to harvest forest areas wisely since they are a valuable source of future income. A commonly owned forest is much more likely to be exploited since no individual owner bears the costs.

Establish Markets for Pollution Rights

Another way to create incentives for responsible care of the environment, consistent with legitimate growth objectives, is to establish markets for the right to pollute. By allowing less efficient firms to purchase pollution "rights" from more efficient firms better able to meet pollution standards, the aggregate amount of pollution can be controlled at socially acceptable levels.

By trading pollution rights, a new firm entering an area could actually result in a *reduction* of pollution. For example, an existing firm might choose to reduce its pollution below governmental standards and thus earn "emission reduction credits," which can then be sold to the new firm. Under an "offset policy," the new firm might have to buy 1.2 emission credits for each 1.0 unit of emissions that it added. Since reductions will be 20 percent greater than additions, the overall air quality would be *improved* every time a new plant entered the area! Similarly, under a "bubble policy," firms cooperate with each other in achieving a stated overall limit on their aggregate emissions.

In studying ways to create proper incentives to improve environmental quality, the main point to emphasize is that in many instances there are creative, practical ways to improve environmental quality instead of imposing rigid regulations that are expensive to enforce and that stifle economic growth. It is encouraging to know that strict environmentalists and those in favor of more growth-oriented policies are beginning to recognize that economic development and environmental protection need not inevitably be seen as conflicting goals.

3. Marginalism

We have learned that negative externalities are an unavoidable by-product of the production and consumption of goods and services. We have also examined various ways to minimize the harmful effects of these externalities on the environment. A key question remains unanswered, however. How clean should the environment be? It is one thing to agree that action needs to be taken to address a particular environmental problem; it is another to agree to what extent the action needs to be implemented.

A Problem in Centerville

Suppose that industries in Centerville have so polluted the local river that it is now useless for drinking, swimming, or fishing and is possibly a serious health hazard. While most people would agree that some cleanup is necessary, they may not agree on exactly how *much* cleanup. Fortunately, the concept of **marginalism** helps students analyze these difficult kinds of problems.

In economics, **marginal** simply means "next" or "incremental." This rather simple concept can help us solve the river problem. Suppose all citizens in Centerville agree that some cleanup is necessary. They hire an environmental firm to analyze the situation and report back to the city council. Table 1 summarizes the firm's findings.

Table 1

Cleaning Up the River

Degree of Cleanup	Marginal Cost	Total Cost	Marginal Benefit	Total Benefit Cleanup
20 %	$10,000	$10,000	$100,000	$100,000
40 %	$15,000	$25,000	$70,000	$170,000
60 %	$25,000	$50,000	$50,000	$220,000
80 %	$50,000	$100,000	$20,000	$240,000
100 %	$100,000	$200,000	$5,000	$245,000

Common sense tells us that, for a given level of benefits, we should first choose the least costly cleanup method, whatever that may be. The firm's data show that 20 percent of the pollution problem can be solved at a marginal cost of only $10,000. The resulting marginal benefit is a significant $100,000.

The data also show that additional methods could be used to reduce pollution by another 20 percent giving a total degree of cleanup of 40 percent. However, the cost of this next (marginal) 20 percent cleanup has increased to $15,000, resulting in a total cost of $25,000. At the same time, the marginal benefit of this extra cleanup has decreased to $70,000, giving us a total benefit of $170,000.

Notice that as the degree of cleanup increases, the marginal cost of the that cleanup increases and the marginal benefit of that cleanup decreases. This makes intuitive sense. Getting the river from 80 percent to a 100 percent pollution-free, pristine condition would be very costly - $ 100,000 - possibly from shutting down some factories altogether and banning any use of power boats. However, the marginal benefit of doing so ($5,000) would not be all that much greater than achieving an 80 percent degree of cleanness.

So how clean *should* the river be? *Economists would say that the citizens of Centerville should continue cleaning up the river as long as the marginal benefits (MB) exceed the marginal costs (MC)*, in this case up to a 60 percent degree of cleanliness. Economists call this the point of "optimality," where MB = MC. After that point, the additional costs of cleanup are more than the additional benefits (See Figure 6). The scarce productive resources used for cleanup would be better used for some other purpose.

Students tend to look at the *total* amounts in their analysis. They often recommend a 100 percent degree of cleanup since the total benefit ($245,000) is greater than the total cost ($200,000). However, that would not be the wise choice, as we have demonstrated.

Automobile Pollution

Another common example that illustrates the concept of marginalism is the case of automobile pollution. One sure way of solving this problem would be banning the use of automobiles altogether. Obviously, the cost to society of doing so would be too great. Instead, our government has mandated the use of pollution control equipment, such as catalytic converters. The logic is that the marginal cost of doing so is less than the marginal benefit to the environment and humans.

To summarize, there are trade-offs and opportunity costs associated with all energy and environmental policy decisions. Thus, it is not wise to implement policies mandating the elimination of *all* negative externalities. Some pollution is inevitable. The key question is *how much*, and that is where marginal analysis is useful.

Figure 6

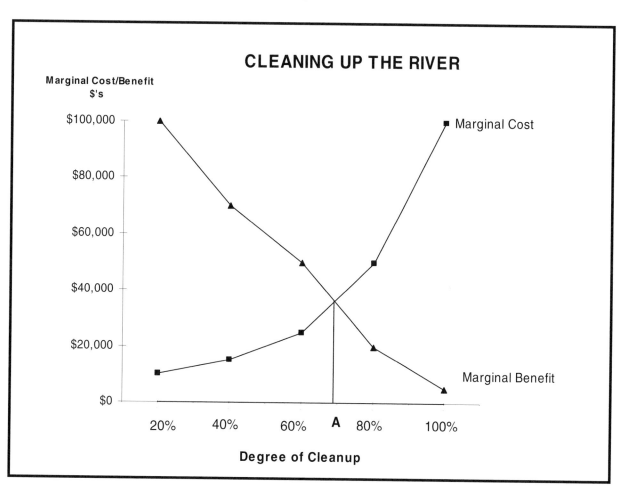

The graph in Figure 6 illustrates the data in Table 1. Notice that the marginal cost increases and the marginal benefit decreases the more the river is cleaned up. After point A, the marginal cost of cleanup exceeds the marginal benefit. Productive resources used to clean the river past point A would best be used elsewhere.

Summary

So how do we solve the complex environmental problems that face us? Below are three points that have emerged from our discussion.

Ways to Help Improve the Environment

1. **Be more sensitive to how our production and consumption decisions affect the environment.** Marginal cost/benefit analysis demonstrates that in many cases, steps should be taken to reduce the amount and change the nature of the pollution entering the environment. In production, this means using technologies that create less total waste and less toxic waste. It also means treating industrial wastes to make them more easily assimilated by the environment. In consumption and production, this means reusing and recycling to extend the life of resources and developing safe and effective ways to dispose of waste.

2. **Develop wise strategies for dealing with spillover costs.** These strategies must attempt to internalize the costs of production so that those who benefit from polluting the environment also bear the costs. These strategies must protect the environment, yet not stifle legitimate economic growth and development.

3. **Use marginal analysis when deciding how clean the environment should be, recognizing that insisting on a state of zero pollution is usually not the best policy.**

All three courses of action above depend on citizens who are sensitive to environmental issues and who are willing to act in an environmentally responsible manner. In our schools, homes, and churches, we must create and foster this important sensitivity.

Part 2: A Decision-Making Model: A Tool for Analysis

It is very helpful to teach students a reasoned, systematic way to analyze and solve problems. This gives students a powerful tool to use in their analysis and helps them to organize their thoughts about issues, instead of merely voicing subjective personal preferences. Using a systematic approach to problem solving also clarifies the trade-offs involved in any solution and reveals the sources of disagreement about various policy alternatives.

A Simple Decision-Making Model

Educators have proposed many problem-solving and decision-making models. The model described in this section is similar to the simple five-step model used in many curriculum materials developed by the National Council on Economic Education. Teachers may wish to use other, more expanded models; however, this five-step model is easy to learn and is powerful enough in analyzing most problems.

The Five-Step Decision-Making Model

1. **Define the Problem.** Analyze the situation. Gather important facts. What is the heart of the problem, the real issue?

2. **List Alternative Solutions.** Taking into account the reality of scarce productive resources, what are some feasible policy alternatives for solving the problem?

3. **List Important Criteria.** What are some of the important values and social goals that will influence the decision? Which of these are most important to you or to the community? Who will be helped? Who will be hurt?

4. **Evaluate the Alternative Solutions.** Use correct economic analysis to evaluate how each alternative "fits" the various criteria.

5. **Choose the Best Alternative (Make a Decision!)** Which alternative is the most desirable? What are the trade-offs among the different goals/criteria? (How much of one goal must be given up to attain more of another?)

Using the Decision-Making Grid

Students use a simple grid to help apply the five-step, decision-making model. (See the Decision-Making Grid Answer Key on page 20.) Alternative solutions are listed vertically on the left side of the grid. Criteria/goals are listed across the top. To complete step four, evaluation marks are placed in each cell of the grid. These marks can vary. For example, a policy alternative can receive a numerical point rating which denotes its ability to achieve a certain goal or criterion (e.g. 1, 2, 3, or 4, with 1 denoting the lowest ability). Or, one can use marks such as "+" (helps meet goal/criterion), "-" (hinders goal/criterion), "0" (neither helps nor hinders), or "?" (unclear). Multiple pluses (+ +) and minuses (- -) also can be used to clarify the extent to which certain alternatives hinder or help attain a goal. It is also helpful to have students write brief comments in each cell, justifying the logic of their marking.

Whatever decision-making method is used, it will help students get a better grasp of the problem and will help them determine a solution. Be careful! The highest score (using points or +/- marks) may not be the students' final decision. It all depends on the importance (weight) attached to each criterion/goal.

Applying the Five-Step Model

Below is a simple scenario describing a community concerned about the increasing pollution in the local lake. The five-step model is used to help solve the pollution problem.

The Case of the Polluted Lake

Middletown had a problem. The town council was receiving more and more complaints from concerned citizens about the pollution in Lake Lemon, on which Middletown was located. For years nobody complained much about the problem, but as the population grew and as new industries developed near or on the lake, the pollution problem clearly became worse. Fish populations diminished, and swimmers also complained about the dirtiness of the water.

An environment firm hired to analyze the situation concluded that the waste water ejected into the lake by a local plastics factory was responsible for most of the pollution. Unfortunately, this plastics factory was the main employer in the town. If the factory closed down or was forced to restrict its production, many people would lose their jobs. The economic health of the town was at stake.

Some citizens, out of a real fear of losing their jobs, suggested doing nothing. Strict environmentalists in town wanted the factory shut down, regardless of the economic consequences. Some citizens wanted the council to set strict limits on the amount of pollution that could be put into the lake. Still others wanted to levy a tax on the number of plastic products produced by the factory and use the tax revenues for lake cleanup. Some citizens said it would be better to tax the amount of waste ejected into the lake, not the plastic products. What should the town council do?

Applying the Five Steps

Step 1: Define the Problem

The problem is that Lake Lemon is becoming increasingly polluted largely due to the waste water discharges of a local plastics factory, the town's main employer.

Step 2: List Alternative Solutions

Several solutions were proposed in the scenario: do nothing, shut down the factory, set limits on the amount of waste that the factory would put into the lake, tax the number of plastic products produced and use the revenues for lake cleanup, or tax the actual amount of waste ejected into the lake and use the revenues for lake cleanup.

Step 3: List Important Criteria

There are many possibilities. To keep our analysis simple, we will list four criteria: Will Clean Lake, Fairness (those benefiting from the pollution pay the costs), Job Security, and Freedom of Action.

Step 4: Evaluate Alternative Solutions

This is the most challenging part of the problem. In the answer grid below, we have used the +, -, ?, marking scheme, with double pluses (++) and minuses (- -) to indicate strong help or hindrance. For example, for the Do Nothing alternative we put a double minus (- -) in the Will Clean Lake cell since doing nothing will continue to worsen the pollution problem. We put a minus (-) in the Fairness cell since doing nothing will harm individuals who do not benefit at all from the factory. (Since many people in Middletown do benefit, a double minus (- -) was not used.) The Do Nothing alternative would enhance job security, so a + + was put in that cell. A double plus (+ +) was placed in the Freedom of Action cell since doing nothing would give individuals the freedom to pollute (or not pollute!) as they pleased, without interference from the town government.

We have completed the other cells and are now ready to make a decision. (You may disagree with how some cells are marked. In a class situation, this disagreement forces student discussion and contributes to a more logical solution.)

Step 5: Choose the Best Alternative

Based on our analysis, some form of tax, either on production or on actual waste, appears to be the best choice. However, as was mentioned above, because individuals weigh the criteria/goals differently, one cannot merely "add" the pluses and minuses to arrive at a correction solution. For example, a strict environmentalist might choose to shut down the factory. For this person, the cleanliness of the lake is by far the most important criterion and outweighs all other considerations.

Decision-Making Grid Answer Key
The Case of the Polluted Lake

	Criteria			
Alternatives	Will clean lake	Fairness	Job security	Freedom of Action
Do nothing	--	-	++	++
Shut down factory	++	?	--	--
Set waste limits	+	+	?	-
Tax plastic products	+	+	--	+
Tax amount of waste water	+	+	-	+

Unit 1

Water Resources

Overview of Unit 1

Water Resources

Introduction

In this unit, students confront the very real problem of the pollution of our lakes, rivers, streams, and groundwater. This pollution occurs because water resources are often commonly owned and, therefore, tend to be overused by businesses and individuals. Students also will confront the difficult question, "How clean do we want our waterways to be?" It may be possible to clean water resources to an almost perfect, pristine state – but would this be worth the cost, especially in terms of job losses and slowing economic growth? To analyze this situation, students will use the concept of marginalism discussed on page 13.

Learning Objectives

<u>After completing this unit, students will:</u>

1. Understand basic facts about water resources.
2. Explain the economic reasons why water pollution occurs and identify policies to correct it.
3. Explain how a policy mandating zero pollution would affect society.
4. Understand that public policy decisions involve trade-offs.

Unit Outline

I.   Facts About Water Resources

II.   Water Resources Vocabulary

III.   Teaching Activities and Key Concepts to Emphasize

IV.   Specific Teaching Activities
1. The Water Cycle
2. The White Glove Test
3. Get the Iron Out
4. Conserving Water at Home
5. Conserving Water Out West
6. Further Investigations
7. Debating the Issues
8. EEE Actions: You Can Make a Difference!
9. Case Study

V.   Answers to Selected Teaching Activities

Facts About Water Resources

Introduction

Water is perhaps our most important natural resource. Without water, life on earth as we know it would cease. During the past several decades, there has been a growing concern in the United States about the proper management of our vital water resources. Water pollution has been a major problem, and recently certain regions have experienced water shortages. Water resource management will continue to be an important public policy issue. Wise public policy requires citizens and decision makers who are knowledgeable about our water resources and who understand basic economic principles.

Basic Information

WATER, WATER, EVERYWHERE: Water is certainly a remarkable substance. In addition to being necessary for life itself, water transports people, goods, and waste; defines political boundaries; cools industrial equipment; irrigates crops; provides electricity and recreation; plays a major role in determining the weather; and is the "universal solvent." Given water's importance, it is fortunate that it is so abundant. Indeed, four-fifths of the world's surface is covered with water - about 340,000,000 cubic miles! However, little of this water is usable since 97 percent is salty ocean water. Another two percent is stored in glaciers and ice caps. In fact, only 0.8 percent of all the earth's water is fresh water that is immediately available for human use. This amount is basically a fixed supply and is all that we have, given current technology.

FRESH WATER SOURCES: The fresh water that is available for human use exists primarily as surface water or ground water. **Surface water** is water that we can see. There are five basic categories of surface water: rivers and streams, lakes, oceans, estuaries, and wetlands.

- **Rivers and streams** often begin as fresh springs in mountain areas. The springs turn into streams and then into rivers. Some rivers, such as the Mississippi, start from ground water sources. Springs are the natural discharge of ground water to the surface.

- **Lakes** are bodies of water surrounded by a larger land mass. Lakes change as they age, primarily by accumulating sediment from surrounding land areas.

- **Oceans** are large bodies of salt water that cover 66 percent of the earth's surface.

- **Estuaries** form where rivers meet oceans. Estuaries are valuable because they are places where many aquatic species live and breed.

- **Wetlands** are low-lying areas that are periodically covered with shallow water. Wetlands are natural filters that preserve and protect ground water quality, help control flooding, and are a breeding ground for many species of wildlife.

Ground water is stored underground. Its importance is illustrated by its volume — over 30 times greater than the volume of rivers, streams, and lakes. Many people believe ground water exists in underground caves. In fact, most ground water is contained in **aquifers**, porous underground areas containing sand or loosely packed granular materials. The size of the material determines the storage capacity of the aquifer (**porosity**) and its ability to transmit ground water (**permeability**). Ground water flow can vary from several feet a day to only inches per year. Aquifers may be near the surface or deep underground. They may be shallow formations or may be thousands of feet thick. About one fourth of all the fresh water used in the United States (one half of the drinking water) comes from underground sources. Nearly 60 percent of Indiana's population uses ground water for drinking water.

WATER CYCLE: The amount of water available for human use is being replenished constantly through the **water cycle**. Water evaporates into the atmosphere in the form of water vapor. Only pure water evaporates — solids, impurities, and salts remain behind. Eventually, the water vapor cools and falls as fresh water, usually as rain or snow. Most water falls into the oceans. The water that falls on land surfaces either flows into streams and rivers, eventually reaching the oceans, or seeps into the ground and replenishes the groundwater supply. Ground water and surface water interact in the water cycle, as ground water partially recharges rivers, streams, lakes, and oceans. The water cycle is a never-ending process that continually renews the fresh water of the earth.

WATER DISTRIBUTION: One of the unique and challenging features about fresh water availability is its uneven distribution. In some countries and in some regions of the United States, there is an abundant per capita water supply. In other areas, water is much more scarce. And yet, human habitation doesn't always correlate with fresh water availability. For example, there is abundant water in the sparsely populated rainforests of South America, but much less water in certain heavily populated regions in the western United States. These arid regions have continuous or periodic water shortages.

Water Management Problems

There are two fundamental problems in the area of water resource management: 1. the issue of **pollution** (quality) and 2. the issue of **availability** (quantity).

WATER POLLUTION: Water pollution is a complex and interesting subject. In general, people want clean water and have strong opinions about water quality. In the 1960s, people became very concerned about the deteriorating quality of water in the United States. Since that time, water quality has improved throughout much of the country. However, water pollution is still a real problem and is the focus of much public concern.

Pollution: What is it? It is important to distinguish between "waste" and "pollution." In nature, all living creatures generate waste. It is best to think of **pollution** as meaning "too much." Too much of anything, including waste products, even if it is **biodegradable**, is not good for the environment. For example, in 1776 the biodegradable waste dumped into the rivers from small farms was not a problem. The same could not be said today. There are more people, and the sheer quantity of such waste would cause a major pollution problem.

Pollution from Nature: Water can be polluted by nature as well as by humans. The most common surface water pollution comes from erosion. Soil particles that enter surface water block sunlight and impair photosynthesis, a process plants depend on to survive. Volcanic eruptions and forest fires cause thermal pollution of surface waters. In some areas, high levels of dissolved salts, irons, calcium, or magnesium may make water unsuitable for drinking or other domestic and farming purposes.

Pollution from Humans: Any time water is used in production or consumption, its quality changes to some degree. If this change is significant, the water becomes "polluted." Primary sources of pollutants are households, industry, agriculture, municipal landfills, and certain government activities.

Types of Water Pollution: There are various basic types of water pollution:

- **Biodegradable Wastes:** Biodegradable wastes, such as sewage and food waste, can harm water supplies because they provide food for oxygen-consuming bacteria. These wastes also contain disease-causing bacteria, viruses, and parasitic worms.

- **Plant Nutrients:** Fertilizers enter waterways primarily from agricultural runoff, causing excessive growth of algae and other water plants. The decomposition of dead plants by bacteria reduces oxygen content and kills certain aquatic populations.

- **Chemical Wastes:** Many different kinds of organic and inorganic chemicals enter our water supplies in a variety of ways. Examples include various toxic wastes, leakage from underground tanks, and pesticides.

- **Heat:** Many large industries use water to cool their machinery. When this heated water is discharged into waterways, it raises overall water temperatures. This reduces dissolved oxygen content and harms certain fish and crustacean populations.

- **Sediments:** Poor soil conservation practices often allow large levels of **silt** to enter waterways. An excessive amount of silt clouds water, limiting the sunlight necessary for photosynthesis by algae and other water plants. When the silt settles to the bottom as sediment, it covers the spawning areas of fish and shellfish.

- **Radioactive Materials:** Despite very stiff regulations about radioactive waste disposal, radioactive materials sometimes enter our waterways, primarily through uranium mining, fallout from nuclear testing, and accidental releases.

Point and Nonpoint Source Pollution: The various types of water pollution can be categorized into two major groups: point source pollution and nonpoint source pollution. **Point source** pollution enters water resources at a particular site, such as waste water discharged from a pipe or a leak in an underground gasoline storage tank. **Nonpoint source** pollution comes from discharges from large land areas. Examples include runoff from croplands, construction areas, parking lots, and urban areas. The distinction requires different public policy approaches to find effective solutions.

WATER AVAILABILITY: In certain arid areas with rapidly growing populations, water availability is a serious problem. In arid regions that rely heavily on agriculture, such as California, the problem is even more acute because of the huge amount of water needed for irrigation. Local and state governments are developing public policies to deal with this problem, which is difficult because of the conflicting interests of groups competing for the right to use the scarce water resources.

Dealing with Water Pollution

Nobody wants polluted water resources. People want their water resources to be clean and safe. But if water quality is so important, why has water pollution been such a problem? Why are solutions to water pollution sometimes so controversial?

WHO OWNS THE WATER? Water can be found throughout the United States; in fact, we have over 250,000 rivers! You have already learned what an important and scarce resource water is to humans. So who owns the water?

In the settlement of America, the government did not play a large role in **property rights**; rather, it was up to settlers to claim their property. Since water was a significant factor in development of towns, the first settlements were usually located near bodies of water. This accounts for the curved shapes of states in the humid East and along the coasts where there are many rivers. The property rights regime associated with this type of settlement is called **riparian rights**, which give the right to use the water to the owner of the land adjacent to the body of water. This method of allocation made sense because those that owned land near the water had easy access. However, the population of the United States has increased since the time of settlement and this form of water allocation no longer acceptable.

Since a riparian right tied the rights of water to the land, the rights could not be separately transferred to people that needed water, but not the land. The **prior-appropriation doctrine** was developed to solve this problem of water transferability by giving the right of the water to the first person to use the resource, regardless of land ownership. This allowed private companies to construct irrigation systems, which helped agriculture and mining flourish in the arid Western states, whose rectangular boundaries are not water-based.

Currently, both state and federal governments play a large role in the allocation of water. In the 1860s, states began to claim ownership of bodies of water, which gave people a **usufruct right**, the right to use water rather than to own the water. This public ownership allowed the government to control the rates charged by companies for irrigation. When it became necessary for water to be transferred across state boundaries, the federal government became involved in water rights to promote fairness and efficiency in regional development and economic growth.

Since 1900, the federal government has built almost 700 dams to provide water and power to the West. Much of the water used by localities and for development is subsidized by the federal government. For example, 81 percent of the cost of supplying irrigation water and 64 percent of municipal water costs are paid by the federal government.

THE PROBLEM OF SPILLOVER EFFECTS: The major economic reason why water pollution is a problem is that most water resources are commonly owned, and are, therefore, overused. For example, a company located on a river has an economic incentive to use the river (or the air) for waste disposal because there is no immediate cost for doing so. This probably would not be a problem if only one company put waste in the river; but if many companies use the river for waste disposal, water quality deteriorates rapidly.

The harmful effects of the pollution of commonly owned resources are called **spillover costs**, or **external costs**. These harmful effects are imposed on other people, forcing these "innocent bystanders" to bear some of the costs of production. For example, instead of incurring the production costs of treating waste water properly, a company can shift these costs to others in the form of polluted water. This is the rationale for government getting involved in pollution control. Through regulation, taxation, or other means, the government attempts to force *internalization* of the negative external effects of pollution. (For a more complete discussion of spillover effects see page 10.)

THE PROBLEM OF SCARCITY: At first glance, improving water quality seems simple enough — the government should implement various regulatory policies that keep people from polluting. Unfortunately, the solution is not that straightforward. Water is required in all production and consumption activities; and any time water is used, its quality is affected to some degree. The only way to guard our water resources completely from pollution would be to stop using them altogether — hardly a feasible solution! The real issue to consider in public policy decisions is how clean we want our water to be. Perfection isn't possible.

At the heart of this issue is the problem of **scarcity**. It takes scarce productive resources (natural, human, and capital) to ensure a safe and clean water supply. These same productive resources can also be used for a variety of other valuable purposes. A community that devotes productive resources to water quality must give up the opportunity of using these resources for other things, such as better roads, schools, and police protection.

HOW CLEAN IS CLEAN? How does a community or society determine how many productive resources to devote to water quality or to any other energy or environmental problem? The economic concept of marginalism helps to answer this question. (See page 13 for a more complete discussion of marginalism.) The basic idea of "optimality" is that, after some point, it is not wise to devote additional productive resources to water quality since the additional costs of continuing to improve water quality become greater than the additional benefits. After some point, it is better to devote scarce productive resources to other valuable purposes. Marginal analysis includes careful consideration of monetary estimates of the costs and benefits of policy options. This can be difficult, especially assigning monetary values to things such as the recreational and aesthetic value of clean water. For different people, these values will vary. Despite the difficulties, marginal analysis gives policymakers their best tool in analyzing energy and environmental issues.

HOW MUCH IS DANGEROUS? Scientists have made great strides in their ability to detect minute levels of possibly dangerous chemicals in our water supplies. For example, in the 1950s, scientists could detect chemicals in water at the part per million (ppm) level. By 1975, this had dropped to parts per trillion (ppt), and recently scientists have found some chemicals at the part per quadrillion (ppq) level! However, these technological advances can complicate public policy decisions. While we now can detect chemicals previously not thought to be in our water supplies, we lack scientific data confirming how these minute quantities affect human health and the environment.

For example, ground water sometimes contains minute quantities of pesticides that leak into the ground. These quantities are usually detected at levels of parts per billion (ppb), a level equivalent to one ounce of chemical dissolved in one billion ounces of water. (One ppb is approximately equal to dissolving one sixth of an aspirin tablet in 16,000 gallons of water, approximately the amount of liquid held in a large train tank car.) Is water containing minute quantities of these chemicals unsafe? In many cases, we simply don't know. However, this illustrates the importance of dosage levels when defining pollution. For example, substances such as chlorine and fluoride are considered toxic at rather modest levels, yet we *add* them to our water supplies to kill harmful microorganisms and reduce tooth decay.

HOW SAFE IS OUR WATER? Since the 1970s, water quality has improved significantly in the United States, thanks in part to federal legislation, such as the Clean Water Act of 1972 and the Safe Drinking Water Act (SDWA) of 1974. These acts charge the Environmental Protection Agency (EPA) with monitoring overall water quality. The SDWA established national water standards called maximum containment levels, or MCLs, for any pollutants that "may" have negative effects on human health. Public water supplies must monitor and comply with these standards. Individuals with private water supplies are responsible for monitoring the quality of their own water. The Clean Water Act and other acts required the EPA to establish national effluent standards and to monitor the amounts of contaminants entering our waterways.

Since 1999, states have been required to develop and implement standards of quality for all of their waters. These values, known as the Water Quality Standards, represent the maximum allowable levels of various contaminants that may exist in the water without causing serious human health problems. To comply with the Clean Water Act, states are required to assess the quality of all bodies of water regarding these standards. If the actual concentration of any particular contaminant exceeds the standard in a given water body, the water body is deemed to be impaired with respect to that pollutant. The state is required to develop and implement specific plans for attaining Total Maximum Daily Loads, commonly known as TMDLs, for all impaired water bodies. These are calculations of the maximum amount of specific pollutants that a particular body of water can receive in one day and still remain within the standard.

Experts agree that many water supplies in the United States are generally safe for their intended purposes. However, this issue will remain a source of controversy since some level of contamination is inevitable, and individuals will disagree on the effects of minute quantities of contaminants that now can be detected.

Dealing with Water Availability

TWO GENERAL APPROACHES: There are various regions in the western United States that have too little water. This is due largely to low and variable precipitation, high runoff evaporation rates, depletion of ground water supplies because of intensive irrigation, and increased demand from a growing population. There are two basic approaches to dealing with water availability problems: 1. increase **supply** and/or 2. reduce **demand**.

INCREASING SUPPLY: There are various ways to increase water supplies. One of the primary ways is to build dams and reservoirs. These collect water and store it for dry periods, provide flood control, and are a source of energy for electric generation. However, dams and reservoirs are costly to build and they must also be kept free from silt, which can disrupt a river's ecological balance.

Water diversion projects transfer water from one watershed to another, but they are expensive and may have harmful environmental impacts. Another alternative is to rely more heavily on ground water sources. This also can be a problem because excessive usage leads to aquifer depletion. Less feasible alternatives include cloud seeding, and desalination (which is quite expensive).

REDUCING DEMAND: There are two primary ways to reduce water usage. The first is to conserve water by promoting better **water efficiency**. Water efficiency measures how much water it takes to do a certain task. Because water has been generally plentiful and inexpensive in the United States, water efficiency has not been a major concern. Industry, agriculture, and households have tended to use large amounts of water. There has been an emphasis recently to improve water efficiency in all areas. Many industries now recycle waste water for reuse and use new manufacturing techniques to conserve water. In agriculture, new irrigation techniques reduce evaporation and seepage. Many households now have water-saving fixtures and devices that significantly reduce water usage.

The second basic way to reduce water usage is through **full-cost pricing**. Because of government subsidies and pricing policies, the price of water is often kept artificially low and does not reflect the true relative scarcity of water. For example, residential water meters frequently use "decreasing block" pricing, which charges a lower rate for successive units (volume discounts for each hundred gallons per week), rather than "increasing block" pricing, where citizens pay more as they use more water. Low prices encourage consumption and reduce water efficiency. In some regions, consumers are not even metered for their water usage. The obvious economic solution is to establish a true market price for water. Politically, however, this can be difficult. Consumers, especially western farmers, depend heavily on supplies of cheap water. Water pricing and the parallel issue of water rights will remain important and controversial issues.

Summary

Is there really a water crisis in the United States, as some news stories indicate? In general, experts agree that there is no immediate crisis in water quality or availability. For the most part, water supplies in the United States are adequate and the quality is suitable for desired purposes. However, average national statistics mask real local and regional problems. Most experts believe that the water management policies of the federal government, which previously focused on national standards, are shifting to accommodate these local and regional needs. As one report stated:

> Because water management problems and concerns are increasingly localized and complex, the focus of policy decision making is now shifting to non-Federal levels. Where nationally consistent policies were appropriate to water quality or resource management in the past, today's problems require more finely tuned responses.... These may take the form of supplementing national policies with flexibility to address local considerations or even of defining what is "national" in terms of diverse regional or local solutions to a particular water management problem.[1]

One thing is certain — water management issues will figure prominently in public policy decisions in the years ahead.

---

1. "An Overview of the Nation's Water," *World Eagle*, (March 1992), p. 33.

Water Resources Vocabulary

Aquifer
Porous underground layers of sand or other granular materials that hold ground water

Biodegradable
Capable of being broken down into simpler substances by the action of living organisms such as bacteria

Effluent
Wastewater that is discharged into waterways (may be treated or untreated)

Environmental Protection Agency (EPA)
Federal governmental agency responsible for making and enforcing environmental regulations

Estuaries
Surface water areas where rivers meet oceans

Ground Water
Water located in aquifers beneath the earth's surface

Marginal Benefit of Pollution Control
The benefit of eliminating an additional amount of pollution

Maximum Containment Levels (MCLs)
Legally-enforceable water pollution standards for certain chemicals set by the EPA under the Safe Drinking Water Act (SDWA)

Natural Pollution
Pollution caused by forces of nature

Nonpoint Source Pollution
Pollution that does not enter surface water at any one place

Percolation
The action of surface water gradually seeping underground

Point Source Pollution
Pollution that enters surface water from one particular source, such as wastewater from a pipe

Sediment
Small soil particles that settle on the bottom of waterways

Sludge
The residue that remains after treating wastewater

Spillover Costs (External Costs)
When harmful effects of pollution are imposed on individuals not directly involved in the buying and selling decisions that caused the pollution

Surface Water
All the water that one can see, including oceans, rivers and streams, lakes, estuaries, and wetlands

Thermal Pollution	When the temperature of surface water is raised to harmful levels by the addition of warmer water
Trade-off	Giving up some of one thing in order to get some of another
Transpiration	The giving off of moisture through skin pores or leaves
Wastewater	Water discharged by users into surface water; may be treated or untreated
Water Cycle	The movement of water in our environment as it goes from liquid to vapor, and back to liquid again
Water Efficiency	Measure of how much water it takes to do a certain task
Water Pollution	Harmful and unwanted effects on waterways caused by contaminants and wastes
Wetlands	Areas periodically covered with shallow water, such as swamps, marshes, and bogs

Teaching Instructions

Overview

The specific teaching activities in this unit do not necessarily have to be done in order. However, it may be best to do the Case Study toward the end of the unit when students have mastered much of the basic information.

Some of the basic information to teach your students is found in the Facts About Water Resources section. Other information is available from a variety of sources. Encourage your students to research this information on their own. The Further Investigations sections suggest a variety of research activities.

Some of the key economic concepts your students should learn are described below in the Important Concepts to Emphasize section. The Key Questions to Ask Students section will also be helpful.

Important Concepts to Emphasize

1. **Pollution and Spillover Costs** — Wastewater discharges impose spillover costs (external costs) on "innocent bystanders." The spillover costs of water pollution, like air pollution, especially arise when no one *owns* particular water resources. Since there is no cost for people or businesses to use these commonly owned water resources, they become overused and polluted. Government intervenes to correct this problem, usually with regulation and/or taxation. The government tries to "internalize" the external costs so that the producers and consumers who benefit from polluting the water resources bear the costs.

2. **The Problem of Growth** — In the Case Study, the cause of the pollution problem was the cumulative effect of the growing number of factories. The individual firms were complying with existing environmental standards, but as overall production increased, the lake was unable to assimilate the increasing discharges.

3. **Growth Versus Protecting the Environment** — These two community goals frequently come into conflict, as they do in the Case Study. Emphasize that protecting the environment will hurt economic growth to some degree. There is no free lunch; it is costly to implement environmental regulations. Usually, any solution involves trade-offs. Communities accept moderate amounts of pollution so that economic growth is not hampered too severely.

4. **Marginal Analysis** — "How clean *should* our waterways be?" This question is at the heart of the issue of water pollution. Some strict environmentalists (like Dr. Johnson in the Case Study) will tolerate little or no pollution. For others, larger amounts of pollution are quite tolerable, especially if it means jobs for the community. Economists argue that it makes sense to clean up water resources to the point where the additional (marginal) benefits of the purer water equal the additional (marginal) costs. Beyond that point further clean-up is unwise, since scarce productive resources could best be used elsewhere. See the more completed discussion of marginal analysis in the Introduction (page 13).

5.   **Making Growth and Environmental Protection More Compatible** — The goals of growth and environmental protection are increasingly being viewed as more compatible. A new idea is the selling of pollution rights. By allowing less efficient firms to purchase pollution "rights" from more efficient firms better able to meet pollution standards, the aggregate amount of pollution can be controlled at socially acceptable levels.

Teaching Suggestions

Do the following activities with your students:

ACTIVITY 1: THE WATER CYCLE. Make sure your students follow all the directions carefully. You may wish to have students write a paragraph describing the water cycle and the places where pollution enters the cycle.

ACTIVITY 2: THE WHITE GLOVE TEST – HOW CLEAN IS CLEAN? In this activity, students learn to use marginal analysis in deciding how clean the environment should be. Essentially the same teaching activity ("How Much Is Enough?") also appears on page 145 of this booklet, where the activity has been modified to apply specifically to the issue of global warming.

ACTIVITY 3: GET THE IRON OUT! Even though this is a hypothetical scenario, it is a realistic one. Some states are considering regulations that would require reductions in iron concentrations in local water supplies.

ACTIVITY 4: CONSERVING WATER AT HOME. Your students will relate well to the issue of shower length! Discuss their answers in class. You may want students to work in groups and present their conclusions to the class.

ACTIVITY 5: CONSERVING WATER OUT WEST. The economic concepts of **shortage**, **price**, and **demand** are presented in this activity. It is important to emphasize that increasing the price of a natural resource is an effective and efficient way to get *consumers* to conserve. A higher price is also the most efficient way to get *producers* to search for new supplies of a natural resource.

ACTIVITY 6: FURTHER INVESTIGATIONS. Encourage students to do their own research. If time permits, let students share information they have learned with their classmates.

ACTIVITY 7: DEBATING THE ISSUES. Students can debate orally or present their views as a written assignment.

ACTIVITY 8: EEE ACTIONS: YOU CAN MAKE A DIFFERENCE! Encourage students to implement some of the suggested activities.

ACTIVITY 9: CASE STUDY: THE CASE OF THE POLLUTED LAKE. Make sure your students understand the Five-Step, Decision-Making Model. (See Introduction, page 17.) You can do this case study as a large or small group activity. Students should use the Decision Worksheet (page 51) and the Decision Grid (page 52) to help them. Discuss the different group decisions.

Another way to complete this activity is to have individual students or small groups of students make presentations supporting the various viewpoints in the case study. Let the rest of the class be the city council and decide what to do.

Key Questions To Ask Students

1. What is water pollution? *(It is best to think of pollution as meaning "too much." All water is "polluted" in that it contains trace elements of various kinds of substances. Water becomes polluted when the quantity of these substances makes water unusable for its desired purpose.)*

2. What is the primary economic reason for water pollution? *(Pollution occurs because no one usually owns water resources. Businesses and individuals can use these resources without paying for them, causing them to become overused and polluted.)*

3. How do governments deal with water pollution? *(They impose regulations and pollution taxes, give subsidies to firms to clean up water resources, create market incentives to encourage firms to control pollution.)*

4. Why is a proposal to entirely eliminate water pollution unreasonable? *(In the first place, it is impossible to eliminate all traces of pollution in water. All water is "polluted" to some degree. More importantly, the additional cost of eliminating increasingly smaller amounts of pollution eventually outweighs the additional benefits of doing so. At some point, we must accept a certain level of pollution.)*

5. In the case study, is Marty and Sam's idea to impose regulations and have employees and owners accept lower wages and profits fair? *(It is fair to the extent that it conforms to this basic principle – the producers and the consumers who cause and benefit from the pollution should bear the costs. It is a reasonable suggestion since consumers would pay a higher price for goods produced by polluting firms, which would receive lower profits and their workers would earn lower wages while still keeping their jobs.)*

Unit 1

Water Resources

Student Activities

Activity 1

The Water Cycle

Directions: This activity will help you to understand the **water cycle**, the process that replenishes and purifies the world's water supply.

Task 1: In the space below or on another piece of paper, diagram the water cycle. On the diagram show at least *three* different types of surface water and show groundwater aquifers. Also show where the following occur within the cycle: evaporation, precipitation, percolation, and groundwater movement.

Task 2: On your diagram, illustrate how pollution enters our water resources.

Activity 2

The White Glove Test – How Clean is Clean?

Overview

This motivating group activity forces students to address the difficult question, "How clean is a clean environment?" Students learn a very important economic concept – that the opportunity cost of continuing to clean up the environment eventually becomes too great. At some point, the marginal (extra) cost and effort required for additional environmental cleanup exceed the marginal (extra) benefit. When this situation is reached, scarce productive resources used for cleanup would best be used elsewhere.

Learning Objectives

After completing this activity, students will understand that:

1. It is costly to clean the environment.

2. Individuals usually clean the environment by doing the least costly activities first.

3. It is too expensive, in terms of opportunity cost, to have a 100 percent clean environment.

4. Individuals differ on their definition of a "clean" environment.

Notes to the Teacher

• Important! Make sure you have enough "polluting materials," since some materials must be left after the first round. You'll be surprised how well 25 students can clean up a classroom in one minute!
• It is also very effective, and easier, to choose a small group of students to do the cleanup activity. The rest of the class can observe and be involved in the discussion.

Teaching Instructions

1. When your students are out of the classroom, litter the floor with a variety of different-sized "polluting materials." Possible suggestions: books, balls of scrap paper, popcorn, pencil sharpener shavings, sawdust, small dots of paper from a paper punch, and dried grits (what people eat down South!).

2. When the students arrive, inform them that a mysterious polluter has littered their classroom, and they have to clean it up. To make the cleanup more interesting, tell the students you have decided to make a lesson out of this task.

3. Students must clean the room in three one-minute rounds. After each round, students must record on the board what they have picked up. By the end of the third round, the room should be "clean."

4. After the third round ask, "Is our classroom environment clean now?" After the students agree that it is, use a white glove or handkerchief and find dusty areas of the room that are not clean. Ask students why they said the room was clean when it clearly was not!

5. Discussion questions:

   a. Are all classrooms "polluted?" Are all environments? *(Yes, all production and consumption result in some pollution.)*

   b. Why did you say the classroom was clean when the "white glove" revealed it was not? *(It was clean enough. There were dust and other tiny bits of pollution, but they were not very noticeable.)*

   c. Why did you clean up the larger items of pollution first? *(It was easiest and it resulted in a cleaner room very quickly. In other words, the marginal cost was small and the marginal benefit was great.)*

   d. Why didn't you clean up all the pollution, including the dust, etc.? *(It would take too much time to clean the room perfectly. The extra cleanliness was not worth the extra effort. Time would be better spent studying, etc.)*

   e. What was the opportunity cost of continuing to clean the room? *(The other valuable things that could be done with the time, such as studying.)*

   f. After completing the first round, was the room clean enough for some people but not for others? Is your room at home ever clean enough for you but not for your parents? *(Yes! One of the difficulties of solving environmental problems is that people have different tolerance levels for pollution.)*

6. Relate this activity to cleaning the real environment. Students should understand that some pollution is inevitable and that it is too costly to make the environment 100 percent clean. After some point, it is better to use scarce productive resources for other valuable purposes instead of continuing to strive for a completely pollution-free environment.

(An original version of this activity appeared in the article, "A Clean Environment, A Matter of Choice," by Robert W. Reinke and Diane W. Reinke, in *The Elementary Economist*, Spring 1989.)

Activity 3

Get the Iron Out!

Scenario: *Water companies in a certain state soon may be facing new water quality standards. The State Department of Environmental Quality (DEQ) is proposing that local water companies reduce the iron content in drinking water to no more than .3 parts per million (ppm). DEQ contends that iron is very detrimental to water taste and odor and also causes rust stain damage. Some DEQ officials also believe that high iron concentrations may contribute to heart disease and other health problems.*

This new regulation would have a far-reaching impact since iron content levels in the state are typically between .5 and 1.5 ppm. Centerville water quality engineer, Stan Miller, claims the new .3 ppm maximum containment level (MCL) will require construction of a filtration plant costing $2.5 million. "Since we only bill 3,500 customers, we estimate this will increase the average water bill from $16 to $25 a month. In my opinion, DEQ is overreacting. There is no definite proof whatsoever that iron causes health problems. My customers are satisfied the way things are now. They don't want higher water bills."

1.   Why do DEQ officials want to impose these new regulations? _____

        _____

        _____

2.   Since there are possible health problems, why not require iron to be eliminated entirely from the water? Wouldn't this be the safest thing to do? Explain.

        _____

        _____

3.   Would you favor the regulations if they raised monthly water bills by:
        $.10? _____ $.50? _____ $2? _____ $10? _____ $100? _____ $1000? _____

4.   Do you think it would be fair for local communities to vote whether or not they want to implement the higher water standards for iron? Why or why not? Explain your reasoning.

        _____

        _____

5.   "Every day we take some risks and avoid others. This balancing of risks and benefits is common throughout society."

        a. List some risks that you take every day. _____

        _____

        b. Could you eliminate some of these risks if you had more money? Explain.

        _____

        c. Do you agree with the statement? _____ Discuss it with your class.

6.   "The dose makes the poison." True or False? Discuss with your classmates.

Activity 4

Conserving Water at Home

1. Many people are saying that we need to conserve our water supplies. Explain what you think it means to "conserve" water. _____

    _____

2. List at least seven ways that you can conserve water at home. _____

    _____

    _____

    _____

    _____

    Do you think people should do these things to conserve water? _____ Explain. Why or why not. _____

    _____

    _____

3. Terry loves to take long, hot showers. In fact, his showers usually last about 30 minutes. His parents think this is very wasteful, and despite Terry's protests, they ordered him to take 7-minute showers!

    a. Do you think this was fair? _____ Explain why or why not. _____

    _____

    _____

    b. Would it be fair to require a 12-minute shower? _____
        A 5-minute shower? _____ What about a 2-minute shower? _____

    c. To really conserve water, do you think it would be fair to ban showers altogether? _____ Why not? Don't you want to conserve water? _____

    _____

    _____

    d. How long do you think showers should be? _____

    e. How long do you stay in the shower? _____

    f. If your water company raised the price of water, would you and your family take shorter showers? _____ Do you think raising the price of water is a good way to conserve water? _____ Is it a fair way? _____ Explain why or why not.

    _____

    _____

Activity 5

Conserving Water Out West

In some western states, getting enough water is a problem, especially where farmers use large quantities for irrigation. Below is some hypothetical data about how much water would be used each day at different prices in an agricultural region of California. This is the **demand** for water. Graph this demand below and then answer the questions.

Demand for Water

Price per Gallon	Quantity Used (millions of gal. per day)
$ 0.10	10
$ 0.08	20
$ 0.06	40
$ 0.04	70
$ 0.02	100

Price

Quantity Used

1.　Explain how water usage changes as the price changes. _____
_____

2.　Suppose a supply of 20 million gallons a day is the most this region should use to protect surface and groundwater supplies. However, suppose the government has set a price of $.04 a gallon to help farmers irrigate their crops. At this price, what is the "excess" amount of water used? _____. Show this amount on your graph. (Hint: First put a vertical line at 20 million gallons to show the fixed, environmentally safe supply.) At what price would an environmentally safe amount of water be used?

_____

Would this higher price hurt farmers? _____ Explain. _____
_____
_____

Do you think raising the price of water is fair? _____ Explain _____
_____
_____

3.　List three other ways the government could reduce water usage in this region besides raising the price of water. _____
_____

4.　If you were an official, would you favor raising the price of water or implementing some of the ways you listed in 3 above? _____ Why? _____
_____

44

Activity 6

Further Investigations

1. Research the water cycle. Draw a diagram of the water cycle, and write a paragraph describing it.

2. Investigate the water supply in your community. Write a short report describing your findings. In your report, diagram how water is transported to end users. Include answers to these types of questions:

   a. Where does the water supply originate?
   b. What chemicals are used to purify the water? What effect do they have?
   c. How much does it cost to treat drinking water? What are the water rates?
   d. What are local water problems? Are water supplies adequate?

3. Research the Save Our Streams program of the Izaak Walton League. (www.iwla.org/sos) Investigate a local stream in your community. Conduct a comprehensive survey, including these types of investigations:

   a. Find the stream width and depth at three locations and diagram the stream's physical profile. Measure stream temperature at various depths.
   b. Test water quality with water testing kits. Collect and graph the data.
   c. Identify types and levels of sediment.
   d. Walk along the stream to inventory pollution problems, wildlife, plants, and recreation potential. Use diagrams or photographs to record your findings.
   e. Collect and identify stream insects and crustaceans.
   f. Collect and identify water plants found in the stream.

4. Investigate watersheds in your community or region. On a topographical map, identify sources of water that make up the watershed (streams, lakes, creeks, rivers, lakes, etc.) Explain water drainage patterns in the watershed. What are pollution problems in the watershed? Has the watershed changed during the past 20 years? What can be done to improve the watershed? Diagram and report your findings.

5. Identify water shortage areas in the United States. Color code these areas on a map. Identify the causes of these shortages and describe public policies that have been proposed to deal with them. Explain controversial aspects of these policies.

6. Investigate water usage in the western United States. Identify the biggest uses of water and how rights to use water are determined. Explain water rights controversies. How do water rates in western states compare to rates in other states?

7. Research wetlands in the United States. How are wetlands identified? Why are they valuable? Describe laws to protect wetlands. Explain why these laws are sometimes controversial. Identify wetland areas near your community.

8. Research water pollution caused by toxic chemicals. Which chemicals are found in our water supplies? How do they get there? Where is the contamination most serious? Identify maximum containment levels (MCLs) for various chemicals. What are some of the controversial issues surrounding chemical pollution?

9. Visit a local wastewater treatment plant. Interview technicians and officials to investigate wastewater treatment. Report your findings, including diagrams.

   a. What is the treatment process? What chemicals are used?
   b. Where is wastewater discharged? How does this affect waterways?
   c. What are the costs of treating sewage? What are sewage rates? How have the rates changed? Why?
   d. What are EPA regulations concerning sewage treatment? How have they changed? How have these regulations affected your community's sewage treatment?

10. Tour a factory in your community. Interview factory managers about water treatment. Is the water recycled? Why or why not? How is wastewater treated? Where is it discharged? What chemicals are in the wastewater? Are the chemicals dangerous to public health? How has water treatment at the factory changed? Prepare a report of your findings.

11. Investigate how water resources are treated in different countries. How do different religious beliefs (such as Hindu beliefs about the holiness of the Ganges River) and different attitudes toward nature affect water quality and management?

12. Investigate careers in water resource management. The two major career categories in water pollution control are (1) environmental engineering and (2) operations. Environmental engineers perform research, evaluate pollution problems and propose solutions, implement and enforce environmental legislation, and work with the public to resolve water pollution concerns. Operations personnel test for water purity, maintain mechanical equipment, inspect water treatment facilities, monitor wastewater flows, and do other technical tasks. For further information about careers in water management, contact the Water Environment Federation. (www.wef.org)

13. Write to state agricultural organizations to find out what they are doing to help keep pesticides and other chemicals out of water supplies.

14. Research the Safe Drinking Water Act (SDWA), the Clean Water Act, and the Resource Conservation and Recovery Act.

Activity 7

Debating The Issues

Debate and discuss these controversial statements:

1. In the western states, especially California, large growers have used low-priced, taxpayer subsidized water to irrigate their farms and increase agricultural production. This practice should be stopped. Farmers should pay higher market prices for water, even if this increases the price of food and results in losses of some agricultural jobs.

2. In some California regions, citizens are not metered for their water. They pay a flat monthly fee regardless of how much water is used. This gives people of all income levels access to the water they need, but it is a wasteful policy. Water meters should be installed and people should pay for the water they use.

3. To protect waterways, pesticides and fertilizers should be banned. Farmers can use organic farming methods.

4. Firms should be allowed to put treated wastewater back into streams and waterways.

5. Water containing minute, trace amounts of certain toxic chemicals is safe for drinking. We shouldn't be worried about it.

6. Water fountains that put minute traces of lead into the water should be removed, regardless of the cost.

7. Farmers should be able to decide whether certain wetland areas on their own private land should be used for agricultural or other purposes. The government has no right to infringe upon this private property right.

8. Lawn service companies should not be allowed to put chemical fertilizers on lawns since small amounts of these chemicals can leak into groundwater supplies.

9. For years, a company discharged a certain chemical into a nearby waterway. The EPA did not consider the chemical dangerous and did not prohibit the discharge. Years later it was discovered that the chemical was responsible for serious birth defects in children. The company should be held liable for any damages caused by the chemical.

10. The question of cost is not an issue when it comes to protecting our vital water supplies.

11. Almost every chemical compound known to man can be safely ingested if the contamination level is small enough.

Activity 8

EEE Actions:
You Can Make A Difference!

1. List and discuss ways to conserve water in your home. Estimate your savings from conserving water. Where feasible, make a commitment to use less water. Some possible ways to improve water efficiency in your home include:

    a. Take short (5-7 minute) showers. When taking a bath, don't fill up the tub!
    b. Install water-saving devices in faucets, toilets, and shower heads.
    c. Don't let the water run continuously when shaving or brushing teeth.
    d. When washing the car use a hose nozzle that can be shut off.
    e. Repair leaky faucets and toilets!
    f. When washing dishes, don't leave the water running.
    g. Water lawns during cool, windless hours, such as early morning.
    h. Hose down cars, garbage cans, bicycles, and other items on the lawn.
    i. When landscaping, choose shrubs and grasses that require little water.
    j. Use drip irrigation systems and mulch on home gardens to improve irrigation efficiency and reduce evaporation.
    k. Keep a jug of water in the refrigerator rather than running water from a tap until it gets cold enough to drink.
    l. While waiting for faucet water to get hot, catch the cool water in a pan and use it for cooking or watering plants.

2. Recycle used motor oil instead of pouring it on the ground.

3. "Adopt" a stream in your community. Organize clean-up efforts to remove trash from the stream. Monitor the stream to make sure the stream is kept clean.

4. Prepare an information exhibit about a local stream in your community. Display the exhibit at shopping centers, PTA and service club meetings, and schools in your school district.

5. Invite water resource experts to your school to share their expertise about water resources. Share the information you learn with students in lower grades.

6. Investigate possible sources of lead in your drinking water at home. If lead is suspected, have your water tested by a local authority or qualified laboratory. Be sure new plumbing or repairs use lead-free materials.

Activity 9

Case Study
The Case of Eagle Lake

Student Directions:

1. In this case study, you will analyze a problem that all communities face – how to keep local lakes, streams, and rivers clean. While much progress has been made in this area, work still needs to be done. In the scenario below, two boys try to solve a pollution problem in their community. They discover that the solution is not as simple as they first had imagined.

2. Analyze the scenario and use the Decision Worksheet and the Decision Grid to help you determine a solution to the water pollution problems.

3. Be prepared to defend your final decision.

SCENARIO

Sam and Marty lived in the small city of Lakeville, located next to Eagle Lake. More than anything, they loved to fish. Usually they caught quite a few fish – bass, bluegill, crappy, and sometimes lake trout. Lately, however, they were catching fewer fish, and they were wondering why.

"Maybe we've lost our touch," said Sam.

"I don't think that's it," replied Marty. "Other fishermen I've talked to are having the same problem. It's been getting worse now for the past two years."

Three weeks later, after the boys discovered some dead fish floating in the lake, they decided to do some investigating. Mr. Nash, who operated the local boat marina and tackle shop, was eager to help the boys. "My business has been affected by the increasing pollution," he complained. "People don't want to water ski and fish here like before. They're going to Lake Shannon, twenty miles from here. I'd be glad to help you get to the bottom of this."

It didn't take long to discover that several local firms were a major part of the problem. The factories owned by these firms had always discharged some pollution into Eagle Lake. However, the amount had always been relatively small and had met the pollution guidelines set by the Environmental Protection Agency (EPA). But recently, increases in production and more factories had caused the total amount of pollution to increase significantly.

As far as Sam, Marty, and Mr. Nash were concerned, the solution was obvious – make the factories reduce their pollution. At the next city council meeting, they submitted a proposal requiring the firms to install newer equipment to better treat the wastes discharged into the lake. This would reduce pollution to the acceptable levels of a few years ago.

One complicating problem was that many local people worked in the factories. The prosperity of Lakeville depended on the incomes these people earned. Sarah Stockwell, a vice president of one of the older firms, insisted that installing the new equipment would be too expensive. "We would have to raise the prices of our products to make a profit," she declared, "and that would cause us to lose customers. We would lose sales to foreign competition. We might have to move production overseas."

Stephen Buckles, a union representative agreed. "I don't like the pollution either. But if these firms can't make a profit, they will lay off workers. This city can't afford those kinds of layoffs. It would hurt business all over the city. It just wouldn't be fair."

Dr. Sylvia Johnson, a professor at Lakeville College, angrily disagreed. "You've got it backwards!" she declared. "It's the firms that are not being fair. Why should the rest of us be forced to live with pollution that we neither caused nor benefit from? The boys' proposal doesn't go far enough. I propose that we eliminate all pollution, even if it means closing these factories. This will cost a lot in terms of jobs and growth, but it will bring Eagle Lake back to its original, clean condition."

By this time, Sam, Marty, and Mr. Nash were quite exasperated. Mr. Nash declared to the council, "I agree that our proposal would result in higher product prices and possibly layoffs. But someone has to pay the cost of pollution. Shouldn't it be those who benefit from the production and consumption of these products – the owners, workers, and customers? If the wages of all the employees who work for these firms were cut back some and if the firms' owners would accept some lower profits, maybe layoffs would be avoided and the firms could still afford to install the equipment. Certainly this is a fair solution."

This comment, of course, created even more controversy. However, the problem had to be faced. What should the city council do?

Decision Worksheet

Directions:

1. Complete this Decision Worksheet and the Decision-Making Grid to help you analyze the problem.

2. In each cell of the decision grid, your teacher may require you to make a brief comment explaining *why* you made a particular evaluation mark.

STEP 1: *Define the Problem.*

_____
_____
_____
_____

STEP 2: *List Alternative Solutions.*

_____
_____
_____
_____
_____

STEP 3: *List Important Criteria.*

_____
_____
_____
_____
_____

STEP 4: *Evaluate Alternative Solutions:*
(To do this, fill in the individual cells in the Decision-Making Grid.)

STEP 5: *Choose the Best Alternative.*

Decision-Making Grid

Name		Class	

Alternatives	Criteria				

Answers to Selected Teaching Activities

Activity 1: The Water Cycle

Task 1: Make sure students have included all required information.

Task 2: Pollution sources: leaks in septic systems and underground storage tanks, runoff from agricultural land and urban areas, seepage from poorly designed landfills, discharges from point sources such as factories, etc.

Activity 3: Get the Iron Out!

1. They contend the iron worsens water quality and may cause health problems.

2. Requiring iron to be eliminated *entirely* would be safest, but virtually impossible. If it were possible, it would be very expensive.

3. Answers will vary. At some high price, students will not want the regulations. In other words, they are willing to accept the slight health risk instead of paying more for water.

4. Answers will vary. Some will think communities should be free to set their own standards and levels of risk. Others may feel that the state has a higher, compelling interest to impose health standards in this particular situation.

5. a. Driving, walking, eating and drinking, breathing pollution, playing sports, etc.
    b. One could buy a safer car, buy water purification devices, get a doctor's check-up every month, buy the safest most expensive sports equipment, etc.

6. True. It is the *amount* of a containment that determines whether or not something is dangerous.

Activity 4: Conserving Water At Home

1. Answers will vary. Most students will say conservation means using only what you need, etc.

2. Possible ways to save water: shorten showers; use turn-off nozzles on hoses; use less water for baths; water lawn less frequently; use water-saving appliances; use water-saving devices in faucets, toilets, and showerheads; fix leaky water fixtures; don't run water continuously while brushing teeth or washing dishes

3. a.- e. Answers will vary. The key idea to emphasize is that conservation is not our *only* goal. If it were, we would not use water at all! In our example, cleanliness and health are also goals, and water helps us to attain them.
    f. The surest way to get people to conserve water (or any other resource for that matter!) is to raise its price. The law of demand is true – other things being equal, at higher prices people will buy less of something than at lower prices. Most economists would say that increasing the price of water to reflect its true scarcity is a fair and reasonable solution.

Activity 5: Conserving Water Out West

1.   As price decreases, water usage increases: As price increases, water usage decreases.

2.   The excess amount listed is 50 million gallons a day. A higher price would hurt farmers since it would raise their production costs. In order to cover their costs, they would need to get a higher price for their farm products. Farmers probably would say that it is not fair to raise the price, especially since they have used low-priced, subsidized water for years. Those especially concerned about the depletion of water resources would say it is very fair making farmers (and consumers of farm products) pay the full market price for water.

3.   Rationing; rules prohibiting certain uses of water, such as washing cars; education programs to encourage people to use less water; selling water-saving devices for water fixtures or toilets at subsidized prices

4.   Answers will vary

Activity 9: Case Study: The Case of Eagle Lake

See the suggested solution. You and your students will probably disagree on some of the marks in the cells. There isn't necessarily a right solution since individuals assign different weights to the criteria. For example, although most people would not take the rather extreme view of Dr. Sylvia Johnson to close all the factories, there are undoubtedly some who feel so strongly about preserving the pristine nature of water resources that they would agree with her suggestion.

Suggested Solutions			
The Case of Eagle Lake			
Criteria/Goals			
Alternatives	**Fairness**	**Effect on Environment (Including Health and Safety)**	**Economic Growth and Jobs**
Do Nothing (Reject boys' proposal)	- Pollution harms others	- - Environment, health and safety hurt	+ + Growth and jobs would continue
Adopt Boys' Proposal	+ Those who benefit bear costs	+ Would help clean environment	- Would hurt growth/jobs
Clean Up Pollution Entirely (Dr. Johnson's Proposal)	? Helps some, hurts others	+ + Benefits environment a lot	- - Very harmful to growth and jobs
Nash Suggestion (Adopt boys' proposal with wage cuts and lower profits.)	+ Those who benefit bear costs	+ Would help clean environment	+ Keep jobs though with lower pay

Unit 2

Forest Resources

Overview of Unit 2

Forest Resources

Introduction

Forest management in the United States has improved greatly since the early part of this century when our forests were often abused. Forest growth today is improving steadily, even in the face of increasing demand for wood products. Nevertheless, there is always a need for better forest management and there are still controversial issues that confront policymakers. Your students will enjoy learning about forests and dealing with some of these issues.

Learning Objectives

After completing this unit, students will:

1. Learn to analyze an environmental issue using a five-step, decision-making model.
2. Explain five basic benefits of forest resources.
3. Understand key facts about forest resources in the United States.
4. Understand that public policy decisions involve trade-offs among goals.

Unit Outline

I. Facts About Forests and Forest Management in the United States

II. Forest Management Vocabulary

III. Teaching Instructions and Key Concepts to Emphasize

IV. Specific Teaching Activities
　　1. Graphing Forest Facts
　　2. Conducting a Forest Survey
　　3. Forest Benefits and Conflicting Goals
　　4. Forest Economics
　　5. Further Investigations
　　6. Debating the Issues
　　7. EEE Actions – You Can Make a Difference!
　　8. Case Study

V. Answers to Selected Teaching Activities

Facts About Forests and Forest Management in the United States

Introduction

Forest management plays a crucial role in natural resource conservation. Our forests are important for many reasons, and issues concerning the management of our forests have received much attention in recent years. Wise public policy decisions concerning our forests require citizens and decision makers who are knowledgeable about basic forest facts and forest management.

Benefits of Our Forests

A **forest** is a dynamic community composed of living and nonliving things which is dominated by trees. Forests provide enormous and diverse benefits to our society and world. Indeed, to sustain a lifestyle beyond a bare subsistence level, forest resources are virtually a necessity. The basic benefits forest resources provide are categorized below into five major groups.

Group 1: Forest Products

Forest products are used in an estimated 5,000 commercial products, mainly comprised of lumber, paper, and plywood. However, trees are also used in the production of resins, waxes, medicines, vitamins, adhesives, lacquers, mulches, various chemicals, dinnerware, electrical receptacles, handles for cooking utensils and tools, textile products, baby food, cattle feed, insecticides, printing inks, asphalt, chewing gum, cement, ceramics, fertilizers, cosmetics, gummed tape, and many other items. Other kinds of special forest products include Christmas trees, nuts, and syrup.

Wood is also a primary energy source and is used by many for heating and cooking. Today, about two billion people in the world are dependent on wood fuel for cooking, heating, and food preservation. Worldwide, almost two thirds of all wood cut is used for fuel. Nationally, over one half of the paper industry's total energy requirement is met by burning wood residues, such as ground wood, bark, and pulping liquors.

Individuals and businesses that grow, manage, and harvest trees and produce manufactured wood and paper products make up the core of the forest industry, which has annual sales of about $230 billion. It employs about 1.7 million people, with an annual payroll of over $51 billion. In 2000, United States exports of paper, pulp, and wood totaled $18.1 billion. Imports were $30.4 billion. Canada ($5.6 billion) is the largest customer of U.S. wood and paper products, followed by Mexico ($2.8 billion), the European Union ($2.6 billion), and Japan ($2.3 billion).

With 56,000 workers, Indiana's vibrant forest products industry is the sixth largest employer in Indiana. Hardwood logs are the most important and valuable products, with 95 percent of Indiana's forests classified as hardwood forest. The industry produced 348 million board feet of saw logs in 2000, up from 289 million board feet in 1995. The most important hardwoods are red and white oak, tulip tree, hickory, ash, and hard maple. Pulpwood production has also grown. The wood residues from sawmills provide 83 percent of all pulpwood.

Group 2: Outdoor Recreation

Forests are places of tremendous scenic beauty and solitude and are invaluable resources for outdoor recreation. They provide places suitable for bird watching, hiking, camping, hunting, and other recreational activities. Many people have jobs directly or indirectly connected with these recreational pursuits.

Group 3: Biodiversity and Wildlife Habitat

Home to about two thirds of all species on earth, forest ecosystems are the world's largest reservoir of biological diversity and are a natural habitat for a wide variety of wildlife. In addition to being a primary food source, forests are sources of cover, giving wildlife protection from adverse weather, concealment for breeding and rearing young, or simply a place to rest.

Group 4: Watershed Protection

A **watershed** is a major land area that collects and delivers run-off water, sediment, and dissolved substances to rivers and their tributaries. Forest watersheds can be compared to gigantic sponges which regulate the flow of runoff waters from highland sources to cropland and urban areas. The water absorbed and held by forest watersheds is used to recharge springs, streams, and ground water aquifers. This absorption process helps control soil erosion, flooding, and the amount of sediment flowing into rivers and reservoirs.

Group 5: Climate Control and Source of Oxygen

Trees and other green plants are the primary source of the oxygen that humans and animals need to survive. The complex chemical process that produces oxygen is called **photosynthesis**. In photosynthesis, carbon dioxide (CO_2) from the atmosphere combines with water (H_2O) in the tree leaves. This produces a basic sugar ($C_6H_{12}O_6$) and releases oxygen (O_2) into the air. Photosynthesis is catalyzed by chlorophyll and energized by sunlight. The chemical formula is:

$$6\ CO_2\ +\ 6\ H_2O\ +\ Solar\ Energy\ ====>\ C_6H1_{12}O_6\ +\ 6\ O_2$$

Young, vigorously growing forests produce vast quantities of oxygen. As forests age, they produce less oxygen. In old, overcrowded forests, more wood may be decaying than is being added by growth. The decaying process may cause these forests to use more oxygen than they produce.

Forest Resources in the United States

FOREST ACREAGE: The United States is blessed with abundant forest resources. One third of the United States (approximately 747 million acres out of a total land mass of 2.3 billion acres) is forestland. This is about two thirds of the forest cover that existed in 1600. To be classified as forestland, an area must be at least one acre in size and contain at least 10 percent tree cover.

Of the 747 million acres of forestland, 504 million acres are classified as **timberland**, forests capable of growing at least 20 cubic feet of commercial wood per acre per year. Approximately 51 million acres of this timberland are reserved forests. These acres have been set aside from any timber harvesting by law under the National Wilderness System and also include national and state parks. The remaining 453 million acres are classified as **commercial timberland**, land that is available and suitable for growing and harvesting trees. Most (58%) commercial timberland is private land. Of the rest, 29% is owned by federal, state, and local governments and 13% is owned by the forest industry. Overall, only about one half of available commercial timberland is actually used for growing and harvesting trees. Portions are often set aside for non-timber uses, such as recreation and wildlife habitat.

Figure 1

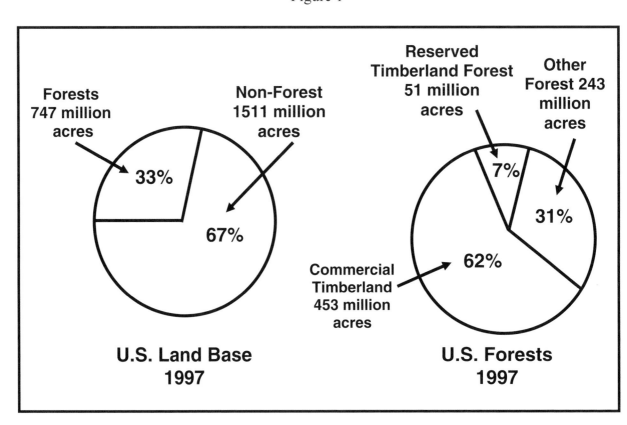

FOREST OWNERSHIP: There are three categories of forest ownership in the United States:

1. Public (federal, state, local, and Indian reservations)
2. Private (non-industrial)
3. Private (industrial)

Figure 2 shows the breakdown. Public land is a significant portion of our nation's forestland and is managed by various levels of government, with the federal government playing the most significant role. Private non-industrial forests consist primarily of relatively small, individually owned woodland plots. Private industrial forestland is owned by large timber companies.

Figure 2

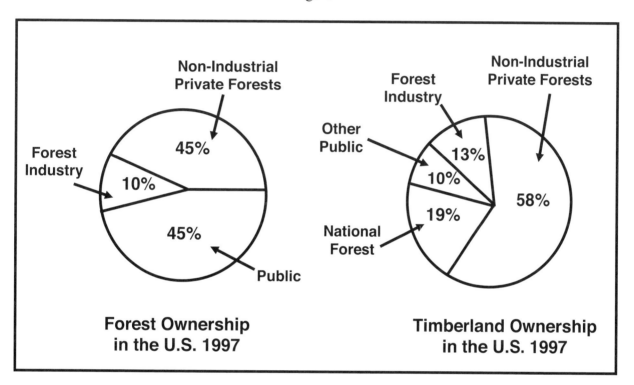

FEDERAL FORESTLANDS: The federal government owns a significant portion of our public forestland. A wide variety of regulations and laws guide the use of these lands. Below is a brief summary of federal lands and their use.

National Forests: Congress established the national forest system in the late 1800s. National forests now cover about 192 million acres. These are "working forests," created to help ensure a continual supply of wood products. Timber harvesting is permitted on some of the national forests. The U.S. Department of Agriculture's Forest Service manages the national forests under the principle of multiple use. **Multiple-use management** means that national forests must also protect and enhance the other benefits of our forests, including watershed protection, wildlife habitats, and recreation. Other federal lands are designated as **set-aside** areas. The purpose of these areas is to promote noncommercial forest uses, so timber harvesting is prohibited. Various federal agencies now manage over 258 million acres of forested and non-forested set-aside lands.

Wilderness Lands: The Wilderness Act of 1964 established the National Wilderness System, the largest set-aside program. Wilderness lands may be forested or unforested. They have no roads, power lines, or other signs of modern civilization. Today there are more than 106.5 million acres in the Wilderness Preservation System. Since its creation, the System has grown almost every year. The passage of the Alaska National Interest Lands Conservation Act added over 56 million acres of wilderness to the System, the greatest increase ever. Most wilderness lands are in Alaska.

Fish and Wildlife Lands: These comprise 96 million acres and are managed by the U.S. Fish and Wildlife Service. These lands are similar to wilderness lands and are set aside as National Wildlife Refuges, Waterfowl Protection Areas, Wildlife Research Areas, Fish Hatcheries, and Fish Research Stations.

Bureau of Land Management Lands: The Bureau of Land Management oversees 261 million surface acres of land, primarily in the western states, including Alaska. These include Areas of Critical Environmental Concern, Research Natural Areas, Outstanding Natural Areas, National Natural Landmarks, Wilderness Study Areas, and Wilderness Lands.

National Park Lands: Another large set-aside program is the National Park System. In 1872, Congress established Yellowstone, the world's first national park. Today, national park lands total 84.4 million acres. By law, the National Park System has two primary goals: to conserve the natural scenery and wildlife for future generations and to let people enjoy the natural beauty of the parks. The national parks' biggest problem has been their success. Annual usage has increased dramatically over the years, often putting biological stresses on park resources.

Forest Growth

OUR GROWING FORESTS: While deforestation is a serious concern in many countries, forests in the United States are in no danger of disappearing. American forests have actually grown in size over the past century, and scientists estimate that our forests now contain 230 billion trees. In the nation's commercial forests, **net annual growth** (timber growth minus losses to harvesting, disease, and insects) is growing slowly but steadily – about .2 per cent a year. This growth is partly driven by higher stumpage prices for cut trees due to the large increase in demand for timber products during the past decades, which provides an economic incentive to continually improve the science of forestry.

There are several reasons for the remarkable achievements in forest growth:

1. *Increased Planting and Reforestation*: Tree planting and reforestation efforts have been very extensive. Each year, approximately 2.6 million acres of trees are planted, an area roughly equal to the size of Connecticut. The forest industry and private tree farmers together accounted for 87 percent of total tree plantings.

2. *Fewer Losses due to Forest Fires*: In the early 1900s, approximately 40 to 50 million acres were lost each year to fires. Today, forest fire losses are approximately four million acres annually.

3. *Increased Forestland Productivity*: Forest productivity, the amount of wood grown per acre, has increased dramatically. This has been due to improved management and care of our forests. For example, in Indiana, a leader in hardwood productivity, the current average annual increase in growth per acre is about 140 board feet. (One board foot is 12"x12"x1.") In fact, "the average annual net volume of growth of Indiana's forests has increased substantially since 1967 and is now estimated to be 268.1 million cubic feet. The steepest increase in average annual net volume growth occurred since the last inventory in 1998."[1]

4. *Engineering Improvements in Building Design*: Engineering improvements in building design have greatly lowered the amount of wood used per square foot of building space. Wood preservatives have also extended the service life of wood.

OLD GROWTH FOREST: The United States has about 9.7 million acres of old growth forest. What constitutes an **old growth forest** varies from region to region, but generally it is a forest with a high percentage of very large trees at least 200 years old. About 8 million acres of such forests are protected within national parks, wilderness areas, and other set-asides. Most of the old growth forests are in the West, although some pockets exist in the eastern part of the country. Where old growth forests are harvested, they are cut at a rate of about 1 percent a year and then are replanted. Set-aside forests not used for commercial purposes will some day become old growth forests.

Managing Our Forests

Healthy, productive forests don't just happen. They require years of careful management and protection. In the past, forestlands in the United States were not managed carefully and in many areas were badly abused and neglected. Although forest management is much better today, there is always a need for better conservation practices and management by all who own or use our forests.

PRINCIPLES OF FOREST MANAGEMENT: A basic principle of forest management is **scientific conservation,** i.e. **"wise use."** This means using forest resources for social and economic benefits without destroying the use of the resources for future generations. This principle differs from **forest preservation**, the restricting of any commercial activity so forests can be passed on to future generations in a natural state. Most public forestlands are managed according to scientific conservation, the main exceptions being the set-aside preservation areas. By federal law, the principles of multiple use and sustained yield must complement the principle of scientific conservation on public forestlands. **Multiple-use management** requires the simultaneous use of forests for timber harvesting, recreation, watershed protection, cattle/sheep grazing, and wildlife habitat. **Sustained yield management** means that forests must provide a continuous high level of forest product output without impairing future forestland productivity. The concept of sustained yield is similar to that of a bank account, where the interest earned is analogous to the growth of forest. To ensure a sustained yield, a timber land owner would

1. Christopher Woodall et al. *Indiana's Forests 1999-2003 Part A.* USDA Forest Service, Forest Inventory and Analysis Program, St. Paul, MN, page 22.

harvest only the tree growth that equates to living off the interest of a bank account and never letting the account go below the original amount of the principal.

FOREST MANAGEMENT VERSUS ENVIRONMENTAL CONCERNS: The forest management principles of scientific management, multiple use, and sustained yield can be interpreted in various ways and sometimes seem to work against each other. An example is the Northern Spotted Owl controversy in the Pacific Northwest. Environmentalists claimed that old growth timber harvests endangered the owl's habitat. Timber companies argued that limited harvesting did not endanger the species but would greatly harm families whose livelihoods depended on timber harvesting.

Despite the controversies and conflicts that take place, the principles of scientific management, multiple use, and sustained yield are considered by many to be reasonable guidelines for the practical management of public and private lands. As one author put it, "Most controversies are not over the principles themselves, but how they are applied."[2]

IMPROVING FOREST MANAGEMENT: The application of wise conservation practices and management by both private and public forest owners has resulted in great improvements in the productivity of our nation's forests during the past 80 years. There has been a growing awareness of the need to manage our complex forest ecosystems more carefully and not to view them solely as a source of timber. More care than ever is being given to preserving wildlife habitat, watersheds, and recreation areas. With proper management, these non-timber uses of our forestland can flourish, even on forestlands used primarily for timber.

There are many resources available for improving forest management. The United States Department of Agriculture and various state government agencies offer consulting services, print information, and many other forest improvement programs. Large forest companies also provide excellent resources on forest management. Another valuable resource is the American Tree Farm System. Established in 1941, the Tree Farm System is an organization of private forestland owners whose lands meet certain forest management criteria. The farms are inspected every five years by volunteer foresters to ensure that the forests continue to be well-tended. Today, there are over 73,000 tree farms, totaling over 29 million acres.

---

2. G. Tyler Miller, Jr. *Resource Conservation and Management.* (Belmont, California, Wadsworth Publishing Company, 1990), p. 391.

Summary

The days have ended when forests can be viewed only as a source of timber. Forest management must take into consideration all of the benefits our forests provide. The good news is that responsible management of our forests can enable us to enjoy all of the many benefits that forests provide — now and into the future. As the U.S. Forest Service states, "When a forest is managed properly, it can provide diversified value with a variety of habitat for wildlife, numerous recreational opportunities, scenic landscapes, jobs which help support a rural lifestyle, clean air, stable soil, high quality water, wood products which we need every day, and healthy trees for the future.[3]

3. *Tomorrow's Forests Begin Today: The How and the Why of Good Forest Management*, U.S. Forest Service, U.S. Government Printing Office, 1988.

Forest Management Vocabulary

American Tree Farm System
An organization of private forestland owners whose lands meet specific management criteria. There are approximately 73,000 tree farms totaling nearly 29 million acres.

Clear-cutting
Forest management technique that removes all the trees from a portion of the land at one time. Forest regeneration is by replanting or natural means.

Commercial Timberland
Land that is suitable *and* available for growing and harvesting trees

Cord
A volume of wood containing 128 cubic feet. Standard dimensions are 4 by 4 by 8 feet.

Economic Growth
An increase in output of goods and services in an economy measured as an increase in gross domestic product (GDP)

Forest Conservation
Using forests to obtain social and economic benefits without destroying their use for future generations

Forestland
Land over one acre in size containing at least 10 percent tree cover

Forest Preservation
Restricting any commercial activity on forestlands in order to leave them in a natural state

Forest Productivity
Amount of timber harvested per acre

Habitat
The native environment of a plant or animal

Market Price
Price of a good, service, or resource as determined by its supply and demand in the marketplace

Multiple Use
Using forests to fulfill two or more management objectives

National Forest
A "working forest" established and managed by the federal government to ensure a continual source of wood. National forests are managed according to the principles of "multiple use" and "sustained yield."

Net Annual Growth
Amount of timber growth each year minus losses due to harvesting and natural losses (primarily insects and disease)

Old Growth Forests	Forests with a high percentage of virgin, uncut timber. Old growth forests usually contain many decaying trees.
Photosynthesis	Process shared by all green plants by which solar energy is converted to chemical energy. Carbon dioxide taken in by the leaves is broken down into carbon, which is retained by the plant, and oxygen, which is released into the atmosphere.
Productive Resources	The various resources (natural, human, and capital) required to produce a good or service
Profit	The amount remaining after all the costs of production have been subtracted from sales revenues
Reforestation	The replanting of trees in forests that have been affected by cutting, fire, or disease
Regeneration	Renewal of a tree crop, whether by natural or artificial means
Renewable Resource	A resource that is replenished through natural processes
Scientific Conservation	The principle of managing forest resources for social *and* economic benefits without destroying the use of the resources for future generations
Set-aside	Forestland that has been withdrawn from commercial use, such as Wilderness Areas and National Parks
Sustained Yield	The timber that a forest yields continuously at a given intensity of management; harvest practices that ensure that the rate of timber harvest does not exceed the rate of timber growth
Timberland	Forestland not withdrawn from use that is available and suitable for producing crops of wood
Trade-off	Giving up some of one thing in order to get some of another
Watershed	Any given area of land which drains or sheds water to the same point
Wilderness Area	A forest area set aside for noncommercial uses

Teaching Instructions

Overview

The specific teaching activities do not have to be done in order. However, you may wish to do the Case Study toward the end of the unit when students have mastered much of the basic information. Some of the basic information to teach your students is found in the Facts About Forests and Forest Management section. Other information is available from a variety of sources. Encourage your students to research this information on their own. The Further Investigations section suggests a variety of research activities.

Some of the key economic concepts your students should learn are described below in Important Concepts to Emphasize section. The Key Questions To Ask Students section should also be helpful.

Important Concepts to Emphasize

1. **Scarcity:** Trees, like all other productive resources, are considered "scarce" since at a zero price there are not enough trees to satisfy all wants for them. This does *not* mean that forest resources are dwindling. In fact, our forests are producing more wood fiber than is being used.

2. **Forest Management Requires Scarce Productive Resources:** Productive, healthy forests require knowledgeable, skilled labor resources and adequate capital resources. Forest managers should understand the latest scientific management principles and have the proper equipment and technology to apply these principles. There is a cost to obtaining these scarce productive resources, as there is in any productive enterprise.

3. **Public Versus Private Ownership of Commercial Forests:** Most commercial timberland in the United States is privately owned (71 percent). Private individuals own 58 percent of this total. Most of the controversial issues that appear in the media involve forest management policies on *public* lands.

    Private forest owners and forest companies have an economic incentive to manage their forestlands intelligently since they will reap the benefits of good management. Poorly managed land tends to lose value, with the owner suffering the loss. A problem in some less developed countries is that individuals may have free access to commonly owned forestlands. This results in overuse since there is little economic incentive for individuals to manage commonly owned forests carefully. An example is the excess cutting of trees for firewood. Tree planting efforts by governments in less developed countries have had mixed results. The *World Development Report 1992*, published by the World Bank, reports that successful replanting efforts have taught an important lesson: "Trees can be a highly profitable commercial crop – but farmers must be given the right to own, cut, and sell them at fair market prices."[4]

---

4. World Bank, *World Development Report 1992* (New York: Oxford University Press, 1992), p. 141.

4. **Wood Prices, Profits, and Incentives:** The market price of wood is determined by its supply and demand and is a reflection of wood's relative scarcity. The market price for wood changes constantly, reflecting changes in supply and demand. In competitive markets, timber producers cannot set the price. They must accept the price that is determined by the market. Profit is the amount left over from sales revenues after all production costs have been paid. It can be expressed as an equation:

PROFIT = SALES REVENUES – PRODUCTION COSTS

Tree farmers try to control their costs in order to increase profits. An increase in the market price also can increase profits. Of course, increasing costs and a decreasing market price will have the opposite effect.

An issue that has sparked some controversy is whether the market price of wood truly reflects the costs of production. Some environmentalists contend that wood producers do not bear the costs they impose on the environment, especially damage to wildlife habitat and loss of scenic beauty. They also contend that wood producers receive direct or indirect subsidies (artificially low harvesting fees, tax breaks, etc.) to harvest on public lands, which lowers timber production costs and artificially lowers the price of wood products. This low price then encourages people to purchase more wood products, putting more stress on our forests.

5. **Paper Recycling:** Students and the general public typically believe that recycling paper saves our forests from destruction. Actually, most trees used for paper production are planted on tree plantations and are harvested like other crops. As the demand for paper increases, farmers plant more trees. Also, much paper is made from wood residues created from the manufacture of wood products or from lower grade trees that have been thinned (culled) in order to improve the growth of the remaining trees. Paper recycling is a good way to reduce the amount going into landfills, but does not save our forests from destruction. Currently, the United States recycles about 42 percent of its paper.

6. **Assigning Monetary Values to Environmental Concerns:** One of the difficulties policymakers face is assigning monetary values when making decisions about the environment. For example, when considering whether to set aside additional wilderness areas, how does one put a price tag on the environmental value of scenic wilderness areas? On this particular issue, some believe that no price tag *can* be put on the value of wilderness. To them, setting aside wilderness is primarily a moral issue, not an economic one. This makes it very difficult for policymakers, who *must* consider economic costs and benefits in their decisions.

7. **Opportunity Costs and Trade-Offs:** Any public policy decision will involve opportunity costs and trade-offs among different policy goals. For example, setting aside more wilderness preservation areas means less wood harvested and, other things being equal, higher prices for wood products. Electing to set aside preservation areas means forgoing the commercial benefits of these areas. Wise public policy requires honest attempts to assess the true opportunity costs of policy options.

Teaching Suggestions

ACTIVITY 1: GRAPHING FOREST FACTS. Students can generate a variety of creative, colorful graphs. Display them on a bulletin board. Your students will probably need to use calculators.

ACTIVITY 2: CONDUCTING A FOREST SURVEY. On the overhead, help your students compile and analyze the data. Your students will be able to manipulate the data they collect in a variety of ways. Discuss the results. Help students come to conclusions about their survey. Encourage them to produce a neat, well-written report. Have them include a graph of some of the data. You may want to collaborate with the language arts teachers.

ACTIVITY 3: FOREST BENEFITS AND CONFLICTING GOALS. Do question 1 of the Forest Benefits and Conflicting Goals worksheet with your students. Encourage very specific uses/benefits of our forests. Discuss the other questions. In question 5, encourage students to write a well-organized, thoughtful paragraph.

ACTIVITY 4: FOREST ECONOMICS. Before assigning this activity, read the Important Concepts To Emphasize section and the Introduction to this booklet to review important economic concepts.

ACTIVITY 5: FURTHER INVESTIGATIONS. Encourage students to do research on their own. If time permits, let students share information they have learned with their classmates.

ACTIVITY 6: DEBATING THE ISSUES. Students can debate orally or can present their views as a written assignment.

ACTIVITY 7: EEE ACTIONS. Encourage students to implement some of the suggested activities.

ACTIVITY 8: CASE STUDY: THE CASE OF THE WILDERNESS AREA. Make sure students understand the Five-Step, Decision-Making Model. (See Introduction, page 17.) You can do the case study as a large or small group activity. Students must use the Decision Worksheet and the Decision Grid from Unit 1. Discuss the different group decisions. Another way to do this activity is to have individual students or small groups of students make presentations supporting the various viewpoints in the case study. Let the rest of the class be the Congress and vote on the proposal.

Key Questions To Ask Students

1. What productive resources are necessary to manage forestlands effectively? *(It takes a combination of natural, human, and capital resources. Especially important is **human capital** – the knowledge and expertise it takes to manage a forest effectively, regardless of the specific management objective.)*

2. In the United States, private individuals own about 71 percent of the commercial timberland. The United States also uses an enormous amount of wood. What has kept our forests growing despite an increasing demand for wood? Why haven't our forests been totally destroyed? *(Private individuals and forest companies have an economic incentive to manage timberland carefully and ensure that forest harvests are replaced through replacing or*

natural regeneration. Completely cutting down forests would mean no future income or profits. On public forestlands, government agencies set regulations to limit excess timber harvesting.)

3. What information does the market price for wood communicate? *(The market price is a reflection of the **scarcity** of wood. A high price means that wood is relatively more scarce. A low price means that it is relatively less scarce. A high price encourages wood producers to produce more wood; a low price encourages them to produce less.)*

4. Does recycling save our forests from destruction? *(Recycling does help reduce the **demand** for virgin pulpwood; however, most pulpwood is planted and harvested on tree farms as a crop. Also, much paper is made from the residues of wood product manufacturing and from lower quality trees that have been thinned from timberland. Recycling does not save old growth forests since timber harvested from these forests is too valuable to use for paper. Recycling does help reduce the amount of waste entering landfills.)*

5. In the case study, what are some of the different goals that are stressed? *(economic growth, jobs, environmental protection, wildlife habitat protection, national security)*

6. In the case study, what is the opportunity cost of using the land in question as a wilderness area? *(giving up the commercial benefits of the land)* What is the opportunity cost of keeping the land as a multiple-use area? *(giving up the benefits gained by making it an unspoiled wilderness preserve)*

Unit 2

Forest Resources
Student Activities

Activity 1

Graphing Forest Facts

Task: Below are tables of various forest facts. Complete the charts by computing the *percentages*. On separate sheets of paper, put these data in graphic format. Create various types of graphs (bar, pie, etc.). Use colored pencils and be sure to label the graphs carefully. If graphics software is available, generate computer graphs.

TABLE 1: Forest Coverage in the United States 1997 (2258 total acres)

Nonforest	1511 million acres	_____ %
Forest	747 million acres	_____ %

TABLE 2: Forest Ownership in the United States (747 total million acres)

Nonindustrial, Private	336 million acres	_____ %
Public Forests	336 million acres	_____ %
Forest Industry	75 million acres	_____ %

TABLE 3: Commercial Timberland Ownership in the United States (453 million acres)

Nonindustrial, Private	263 million acres	_____ %
Public Forests	131 million acres	_____ %
Forest Industry	59 million acres	_____ %

TABLE 4: Timberland Ownership in Indiana (4,296 thousand acres)

Nonindustrial, Private	3,743 thousand acres	_____ %
Public Forests	535 thousand acres	_____ %
Forest Industry	18 thousand acres	_____ %

TABLE 5: Forest Planting on Public and Private Lands (Acres)

	Public	Nonindustrial Private	Forest Industry	Total United States
1970	392,111	763,342	763,344	1,576,797
1980	498,837	595,730	1,168,637	2,263,397
1990	473,754	1,200,166	1,187,637	2,861,557
1998	271,391	1,257,973	1,095,317	2,624,681

Activity 2

Conducting a Forest Survey

Student Instructions: Complete the following tasks:

Task 1: Each person in your class must survey (interview) at least five people about forests and forest management. Only one of these people can be another student in your school. Use the survey form your teacher will give you.

Task 2: Collect and compile the data that your class collects. Put the data in table format. Discuss the results with your teacher and classmates.

Task 3: Write an individual report describing the results of your class survey. In your report, include some mathematical analysis (percentages, etc.) and identify differences in responses based on age and sex. Conclude your report with a summary paragraph describing the general knowledge of the respondents about forest and forest management. Below is a sample outline of an individual report.

Sample Outline of an Individual Report

I.   Description of forest survey project

II.   Data collection

    A. How data were collected
    B. General description of those interviewed

III.   Data analysis

    A. Overall data results in table format
    B. Mathematical analysis

        1. Differences in survey responses based on sex, age, etc.
        2. Graphs illustrating mathematical analysis
        3. Discussion of other survey findings

IV.   Summary paragraph describing survey results and general knowledge of respondents about forests and forest management

Forest Survey Form

Respondent Number #		Respondent Sex		
Respondent age (circle one) under 21	21-35	36-50		over 50
1. How important are our forests to our country?	Very Important	Somewhat Important		Not Very Important
2. Commercial timberland is forestland that is available for growing and harvesting trees. In the United States, who owns most of this land?	Government	Forest Industry		Private Individuals
3. Which level of government plays the largest role in managing public forestland?	Federal	State		Local
4. Are forest and timber resources in the United States declining, staying about the same, or increasing?	Declining	Staying About the Same		Increasing
5. "Wilderness" is land set aside for noncommercial use, where there are no roads, permanent building, etc. Should the United States set aside more wilderness areas?	Yes	Maybe		No
6. Should the United States set aside more wilderness areas if it means higher prices for wood products and other natural resources and the loss of jobs for some timber workers?	Yes	Maybe		No
7. Can forestland that is used for timber harvesting still offer adequate protection for wildlife inhabitants?	Yes	Maybe		No
8. The world's largest producer of forest products is:	United States	Russia		Canada
9. The United States currently recycles about what percentage of its paper?	6% 15%		27%	42%

Forest Survey Final Data Sheet

Survey Question	Respondent Age			
	under 21	21-35	36-50	Over 50
1. Very Important				
Somewhat Important				
Not Very Important				
2a. Government				
Forest Industry				
Private Individuals				
2b. Government				
Forest Industry				
Private Individuals				
3. Federal				
State				
Local				
4. Declining				
Staying Same				
Increasing				
5. Yes				
Maybe				
No				
6. Yes				
Maybe				
No				
7. Yes				
Maybe				
No				
8. United States				
Russia				
Canada				
9. 6%				
15%				
27%				
42%				

Activity 3

Forest Benefits and Conflicting Goals

1. Brainstorm the various uses/benefits of our forests with your teacher and classmates. Make a list of the benefits on the board or overhead projector.

2. Categorize the various forest uses/benefits into the five groups listed below.

Forest Products	Recreation	Wildlife Habitat	Watershed Protection	Source of Oxygen

3. Which uses/benefits *could* be in conflict with one another?

   _____

   _____

4. Do these uses *have* to be in conflict with each other?
   Explain. _____

   _____

5. Explain how forest *conservation* differs from forest *preservation.*

6. Our national forests are "working forests." They were created to make sure that the United States has a continuous supply of wood products. These forests must also be conserved using the multiple-use and sustained yield forest management principles.

   a. Research the job requirements of a manager of a national forest. List these requirements on the back of this worksheet.

   b. Suppose you were the manager of a national forest. On the back of this worksheet, write a paragraph describing some of the difficulties you might have fulfilling the requirements of your job. In your paragraph, describe how these difficulties can be overcome.

Activity 4

Forest Economics

1. Managing a forest for multiple use requires great expertise and many **productive resources** (natural, human, and capital). Read the following scenario and fill in the box below.

Scenario: You own a 200-acre hardwood tree farm. Your goal is not only to sell your timber for a profit, but also to protect wildlife habitats and the watershed and to preserve recreational activities, such as hunting, camping, and hiking. What specific types of **productive resources** would you need to manage your tree farm effectively? List at least five in each category below.

Natural Resources	Human Resources	Capital Resources

2. What is the **market price** of a good or service? _____
    _____
    _____

3. The **market price** of a good or service, like hardwood timber, is not fixed. It fluctuates constantly according to changes in **supply** and **demand**. In the situations below, indicate whether the market price would *increase* or *decrease*.

Situation	Market Price Will:	
1. Wood supply does not change, but demand increases.	Increase	Decrease
2. Wood demand does not change, but supply increases.	Increase	Decrease
3. Wood supply does not change, but demand decreases.	Increase	Decrease
4. Wood demand does not change, but supply decreases.	Increase	Decrease

4. Define **profit.** Also write the definition as a mathematical equation.
    _____
    _____

5. Suppose you cannot cut and sell more trees and you cannot get a higher **market price** for your timber. Based on your mathematical equation in question 4 above, what is the only way to increase your profits? _____ What are some specific ways to do this?
    _____
    _____

Activity 5

Further Investigations

1. Research some forest management careers. Possibilities include forester, land use planner, water specialist, timber manager, wildlife biologist, ecologist, botanist, and recreational specialist. Research education and training requirements, salary, and projected job openings. Report findings to the class. Invite forest management professionals to your class to share their career experiences.

2. Research all aspects of the Indiana hardwood industry. Prepare a report describing the economic impact of the industry, its extent and location in the state, hardwood ownership, types of hardwoods harvested, markets for hardwood, environmental impact, and forest management techniques. Visit a hardwood tree farm and discuss these aspects of the industry with the owner.

3. Visit a tree farm or public forest. Observe the various timber stand improvement and management practices used by the staff to improve the productivity and environmental quality of the forests. Take photographs. Prepare a report describing your findings.

4. Design a forest conservation area on a site near your school where hardwood trees can be planted and harvested in future years. Research what trees would grow best at your site. Also research the economic value of various hardwoods, such as cherry, walnut, maple, hickory, tulip, and oak, before deciding what to plant. Design an environmental impact plan to make sure that other forest uses/benefits are considered.

5. Walk through a forest and categorize the trees you find in a certain area. Collect leaves to help identify the trees. Also identify animals that use these trees as a habitat. Prepare a report of your findings.

6. Interview an Indiana Department of Natural Resources state forester to learn about Indiana forests, including national forests, wilderness areas, state forests, private tree farms, wildlife management, watershed protection, economic value of Indiana forests, forest management practices, and timber harvesting techniques.

7. Research clear-cutting practices of logging operators in the northwest. Explain the impact of such practices. Why are they used? Can clear-cutting be beneficial to forests? Can clear-cutting possibly hurt forests? Why isn't clear-cutting used extensively in Indiana?

8. Prepare a report on the American Tree Farm System, an association of over 70,000 individual tree farm owners who must meet certain minimum standards in forest management. For information see www.treefarmsystem.org.

9. Prepare a short report on the various national set-aside areas in the United States. Include descriptions of national forests, national parks, wilderness areas, national wildlife refuges, areas of critical environment concern, waterfowl protection areas, and wildlife research areas. Identify and color major set-aside areas on a blackline map of the United States.

10. Research how the Indiana hardwood industry has changed during the past 50 years. Write a report and include graphs showing major trends.

11. Research how the national timber industry has changed during the past 60 years. Analyze such things as timber growth and volume, timber revenues, exports and imports, regional harvesting and planting differences, changes in forest management techniques, and changes in forestry employment. Include graphs illustrating these changes in your report.

12. Identify Indiana state forests on a state map. Identify forest acreage, locations, and recreational facilities. Draw a map showing Indiana state forests and recreation areas.

13. Research the paper recycling industry in the United States. Prepare a report identifying paper recycling growth and current trends, quantities recycled, difficulties in matching supply and demand, market prices for various kinds of paper, recycling goals of various states and the paper industry, and virgin wood requirements in new paper.

14. Prepare a report on the Northern Spotted Owl controversy in the northwest. Gather facts, summarize the arguments of the various sides in the controversy, and take a position of your own on this issue. Present your conclusions to the class for discussion and debate.

15. Find advertisements or announcements on forest environmental issues made by various industry and environmental groups. Analyze these statements carefully. What techniques do they use to influence your thinking? Pay attention to the types of vocabulary used and accompanying pictures of artwork. Which statements are most effective? Why? Are they truthful? Why or why not? Put these statements in a notebook along with your analysis.

16. Research some or all of the following forestry management terms and practices: multiple use, even-aged management, uneven-aged management, sustained yield, forest management plan, tree inventory, intermediate management, clear-cutting, shelterwood cutting, seed-tree cutting, whole-tree harvesting, timber stand improvement, pruning, and thinning.

17. Research what role fire ecology plays in maintaining forest types.

18. Contact the Indiana Department of Natural Resources to find out how purchasing a Christmas tree can help the environment! See www.in.gov/dnr.

Activity 6

Debating the Issues

Debate these statements:

1. Mineral and oil exploration in potential wilderness areas in western states should be encouraged to make sure the United States does not set aside forestlands that contain valuable oil and mineral deposits. We must lessen our dependence on foreign oil!

2. Clear-cutting is a useful and effective forestry practice which should be allowed in state and national forests.

3. The federal and state governments should set aside as much pristine wilderness area as possible, even if this means higher wood prices because of reduced future wood supplies.

4. To help families and communities who depend on the timber industry, limited old growth timber harvesting in the northwest should continue, even if this means possibly harming the habitat of the Northern Spotted Owl.

5. The best way to increase timber production is to keep as much forestland as possible in private hands.

6. Protecting our forests and environment is basically a moral issue, not an economic one.

7. To ensure a continuous supply of wood products in the future, the United States government should purchase more timberland, taking it out of private ownership.

8. To help save our forests, the government should mandate more paper recycling.

9. There should be no timber cutting at all in national forests. All timber production should come from private forestlands.

10. To help reduce our dependence on foreign oil, people should be encouraged to rely more on wood to heat their homes.

Activity 7

EEE Actions:
You Can Make a Difference

1. Plant at least one tree at your home or in your community.

2. Where practical, use both sides of paper when taking notes and writing reports. Calculate how many sheets of paper you will save in one year and how many your school will save if all students participate. Calculate the number of trees saved in one year if all students in your school participated.

3. Become a "tree expert" by interviewing forestry professionals and researching/studying forestry management materials. Adopt an elementary classroom and volunteer to teach the students about the economic and environmental value of trees.

4. Invite a panel of experts to your school (forester, economist, environmentalist, etc.) to discuss their knowledge about controversial issues such as clear-cutting, protection of the Northern Spotted Owl, or controlled burning in national forests.

5. Work with someone who owns some forestland to help manage some of their land more effectively. Manage the forestland to encourage timber, wildlife, recreation, and watershed benefits.

6. Create uses for old newspapers and other papers that are generally thrown away.

7. Where feasible, encourage paper recycling in your school and community.

Activity 8

Case Study

The Case of the Wilderness Area

Student Directions:

1. In this case study, you will decide whether the government should designate more land as wilderness area. You will discover that there are important trade-offs that can make this issue very controversial.

2. Your teacher will give you a Decision Worksheet and a Decision Grid. Read the case study carefully and decide what Congress should do. Be prepared to defend your decision!

SCENARIO

A controversy is brewing on the floor of the House of Representatives. It concerns House Bill 190, a bill that sets aside 280,000 acres of national forest in southern Alaska as new wilderness areas. As defined in the Wilderness Act of 1964, wilderness areas cannot be used for any commercial use. They must remain in a natural state, where "man himself is a visitor who does not remain." The new set-aside would be called the Silver River National Wilderness Area. Environmental groups have been lobbying for this bill for years and believe that they have enough votes for passage.

At the center of the controversy is Representative Marlene Timmons of Massachusetts, the bill's sponsor. She is known for her support of environmental causes and has argued strongly for its passage. "It is crucial that we protect public lands from economic development," she emphasized. "We must preserve and protect the natural scenic beauty, the peace and solitude, and the varied animal habitats of our forests. They are priceless heritage that can never be replaced. We have a duty to pass on these unspoiled wilderness areas to future generations."

Arnold Wagner of the American Natural Resources Council disagreed strongly. "There is nothing wrong with setting aside certain wilderness areas. However, this particular land has tremendous economic value. Right now the land is producing valuable timber and providing jobs for families in nearby small towns. There are other valuable minerals on this land, and oil company geologists believe that there are also significant oil reserves. If this bill is passed, energy and other natural resource companies will not even be able to *explore* the area, much less develop it! Zero environmental damage is not possible, but we have shown that we can get timber and other natural resources and still keep damage to a minimum. This land must remain classified as a multiple-use forestland area."

Sylvia White of the Alaskan Environmental League disagreed vehemently. "Even minimal environmental damage is unacceptable for a wilderness area. Anyway, there is plenty of land for economic development. Many of our existing wilderness areas are becoming overused by the many people who use them for camping, sightseeing, and backpacking. If we don't preserve more wilderness soon there will be none left. We must act *now*, even if we give up some economic benefits."

"That's easy for you to say," responded Representative Allen Connally. His Alaska congressional district included the towns and families affected by the wilderness set-aside. "There's no doubt that some people are going to lose timber jobs if this bill passes. Also, reducing the supply of timber will increase wood prices for all consumers. That especially hurts people with lower incomes. There will also be great economic loss to the people of my district if oil companies cannot tap these oil reserves. Don't forget, this oil will help reduce our growing dependence on foreign oil."

Representative Phillip Strong of Illinois sought a compromise solution by proposing an amendment to H.B. 190. The amended bill would still set aside the area as wilderness, which would stop all timber harvesting. However, natural resources exploration could continue. If

significant resources were found, the area would then be open to some commercial development. "This is a proposal we can all accept," he stated confidently.

He was surprised at the continued disagreement. Representative Timmons was adamant. "Your proposal will leave the door wide open to development. We need to set aside this land completely and preserve it for future generations. Isn't this more important than short-term economic gain?" Mr. Wagner was also dissatisfied with Representative Strong's proposal. "We're still hurting timber families," he argued. "And if the explorations discover oil and other valuable minerals, the environmentalists will fight us tooth and nail to halt development. We must keep the Silver River lands open as a multiple-use area. Our economic and national security depend on it."

This touched off another round of heated discussion. The vote is tomorrow. What should Congress do?

Answers to Selected Teaching Activities

Activity 1: Graphing Forest Facts

Percents have been rounded to the nearest whole number.

Table 1:
Nonforest	67%
Forest	33%

Table 2:
Nonindustrial, private	45%
Public Forests	45%
Forest Industry	10%

Table 3:
Nonindustrial, private	58%
Public Forests	29%
Forest Industry	13%

Table 4:
Nonindustrial, private	87%
Public Forests	12%
Forest Industry	<1%

Table 5: There are no blanks to fill out. Students can do various types of graphs showing the data in a variety of ways.

Activity 2: Conducting A Forest Survey

Some correct survey responses are: (2.) Private individuals (3.) Federal Government (4.) Increasing (8.) United States (9.) 42%

Activity 3: Forest Benefits and Conflicting Goals

1. and 2. Answers will vary. Be sure to identify *specific* examples that would be categorized under the five groups. For example, under forest products, identify specific products that come from wood (e.g., plywood, chewing gum, furniture, lawn mulch). Under recreation, list various types of recreation, such as hiking, camping, bird watching, hunting, etc.

3. Examples include excessive clear-cutting to get wood products conflicting with using forests to protect water run-off, or forest harvesting to get timber for houses conflicting with protection of certain endangered wildlife species.

4. Not necessarily. With proper conservation practices and careful forest management, forests can provide multiple uses/benefits.

5. Forest **conservation** means using forests to obtain their social and economic benefits without destroying their use for future generations. **Preservation** means restricting any commercial use in forests and preserving them in a "pristine," natural condition.

6.a. Students will identify a variety of job requirements.

6.b. Encourage thoughtful, careful analysis. Coordination with the language arts teacher could be helpful.

Activity 4: Forest Economics

1. Answers will vary. Below are some possibilities.

   Natural Resources: air, water, sunlight, various minerals needed for forest growth

   Human Resources: various types of work/jobs needed, such as forester, biologist, logger, truck driver, forest planner, tree planter, etc.

   Capital Resources: any kind of tool or equipment, such as trucks, chain saws, climbing belts, tree planting equipment, hard hats, etc.

2. The **market price** is the price of a good or service as determined by its **supply** and **demand**. The market price of a good or service reflects its relative **scarcity.**

3.a. increase b. decrease c. decrease d. increase

4. **Profit** is the amount left over to a business after subtracting all the production costs from all the sales revenues.

   Equation: Profit = Total Revenues (Sales Revenues) – Total Costs

5. Since no more wood can be cut and sold and the market price is not higher, **total revenues** (sales revenues) will not increase. The only way to increase profits is to lower costs. This means better forest management, including using better seeds, more efficient capital equipment, better harvesting techniques, better disease and insect control techniques, etc. **Profit** can be an economic incentive for more efficient forest management.

Activity 8: Case Study: The Case of the Wilderness Area

Below is a suggested Solution Grid. You or your students may disagree with some of the marks, especially the cells under the Protect the Environment and Effect on Wildlife Habitats criteria. Some could say that multiple use will affect the environment negatively, while others will argue that there might be a slight disruption of the environment, but the overall impact would be very minimal. Passing H.B. 190 affects wood prices negatively (-) since, other things being equal, it reduces wood supply and tends to raise wood prices. *There isn't necessarily a right answer to the case study, since students will weigh the criteria differently.*

Suggested Answer Key

<table>
<tr><th colspan="6">The Case of the Wilderness Area</th></tr>
<tr><th colspan="6">Criteria</th></tr>
<tr>
<th>Alternatives</th>
<th>Jobs and Economic Growth</th>
<th>Effect on the Environment</th>
<th>National Security</th>
<th>Effect on Wood Prices</th>
<th>Effect on Wildlife Habitats</th>
</tr>
<tr>
<td>Pass HB 190 (Set aside Wilderness Area.)</td>
<td>- -</td>
<td>+ +</td>
<td>-</td>
<td>-</td>
<td>+ +</td>
</tr>
<tr>
<td>Reject HB 190 (Leave area as Multiple Use.)</td>
<td>+ +</td>
<td>?</td>
<td>+</td>
<td>+</td>
<td>?</td>
</tr>
<tr>
<td>Pass HB 190 With Amendment (Strong Proposal)</td>
<td>?</td>
<td>?</td>
<td>+</td>
<td>-</td>
<td>+</td>
</tr>
</table>

Unit 3

Renewable Energy Resources

Overview of Unit 3

Renewable Energy Resources

Introduction

For several reasons, there has been renewed interest in the topic of renewable energy. One reason has been the increase in the price of oil and natural gas and the perceived vulnerability of the United States to an increasing dependence on foreign energy supplies. Higher energy prices and citizens' concerns about environmental quality have sparked interest in non-fossil fuel sources of energy, such as wind, solar, and nuclear power. What are the advantages and disadvantages of different sources of energy? Will we run out of energy? How much do fossil fuels damage the environment? Is it wise to always maximize one's energy efficiency? Your students will enjoy studying the answers to these and other interesting questions.

Learning Objectives

After completing this unit students will be able to:

1. Identify advantages and disadvantages of different energy sources.
2. Apply different economic concepts to energy issues.
3. Explain various ways to conserve energy.

Unit Outline

    I   Facts About Energy Resources

    II.   Renewable Energy Vocabulary

    III.   Teaching Instructions and Key Concepts to Emphasize

    IV.   Specific Teaching Activities

         1. Renewable Energy Basics
         2. Graphing Energy Facts
         3. Trends in Research and Development (R & D) Spending
         4. Energy Efficiency
         5. Further Explorations
         6. Let's Talk It Over
         7. EEE Actions – You Can Make a Difference!
         8. Case Study – The Case of the Outdoor Lab

    V.   Answers to Selected Teaching Activities

Facts About Renewable Energy

Introduction

In the 1970s and early 1980s, there was great national interest in energy policy and energy conservation. This was primarily due to the huge increase in the price of oil caused by reductions in oil supplies as a result of the OPEC oil embargo in 1973 and the Iranian hostage crisis in 1979. The higher price for oil spurred private and governmental development of renewable energy sources, such as solar power, wind, geothermal, and biomass. In the late 1980s, however, our national commitment to renewable energy waned as the higher price of oil plummeted. Neither the government nor consumers were willing to invest in more costly renewable energy sources and programs when nonrenewable fossil fuels were relatively inexpensive.

In recent years, there has been renewed interest in the issue of energy, especially renewable energy. This interest has resulted from several factors: increasing energy prices, particularly oil; environmental concerns, especially the burning of fossil fuels, which many believe contributes significantly to acid rain and global warming; and the United States' increasing dependence on foreign oil, highlighted by the wars in the Persian Gulf. Further complicating the situation is the fact that research and development (R&D) of renewable energy sources can be expensive.

Public policy issues involving energy have tremendous economic implications. To ensure wise public policy, citizens and decision makers must not only understand basic facts about energy sources, but also must know how to apply basic economic concepts in their analysis of energy issues.

Energy Basics

MEASURING ENERGY: **Energy** can be defined as the capacity to do work. The unit of measurement used to express the heat contained in energy resources is called a **British thermal unit** or **Btu.** One Btu is the heat energy needed to raise the temperature of one pound of water one degree Fahrenheit. A Btu is quite small. For example, if allowed to burn completely, a wooden kitchen match gives off one Btu of energy. A quad is used to measure very large amounts of energy. A **quad** is equal to one quadrillion (1,000,000,000,000,000) Btu's. The United States uses an enormous amount of energy – about one quad of energy every 3.9 days!

ENERGY SOURCES: There are many **primary energy sources** used in the United States, including petroleum, coal, natural gas, nuclear, hydropower, propane, geothermal, wind, solar, and biomass. Figure 1 shows the breakdown by energy source.

Figure 1

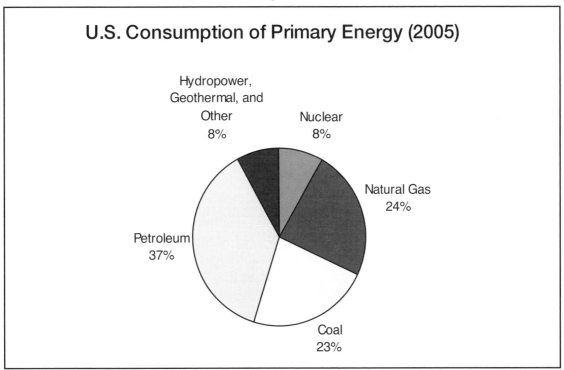

These primary energy sources are classified as renewable or nonrenewable. **Renewable energy** sources are those that can be replenished quickly or that are nondepletable. Examples include solar, hydropower, wind, geothermal, and biomass. **Nonrenewable energy** sources are finite. Examples are nuclear energy and fossil fuels, such as coal, petroleum, and natural gas.

ELECTRICITY: Electricity is a **secondary energy source**, which means that we must use primary sources to produce it. According to the Energy Information Administration of the U.S. Department of Energy, "more than one-third of the primary energy in the nation is used to generate electricity." (www.eia.doe.gov/cneaf/electricity/page/prim2/chapter2.html) Coal, nuclear, hydropower, natural gas, and petroleum are the top five primary sources for producing electricity, with coal (more than one-half) as the largest source (www.eia.doe.gov/kids/energyfacts/sources/non-renewable/coal.html). Unlike the primary energy sources, electricity is not classified as renewable or nonrenewable.

TRENDS IN UNITED STATES ENERGY CONSUMPTION: As the economy and population of the United States have grown, so has energy consumption. However, this increase has been marked by remarkable increases in **energy efficiency**. For example, in 2002, the United States consumed about 25-30 percent more energy annually than during the 1970s, while population grew by 30 percent. However, the value of the nation's real **gross domestic product - GDP** (the total value of all the final goods and services produced in the economy in a year) was 80 percent higher! The United States has improved its energy/GDP ratio as fast or faster than other developed countries. This improvement in energy efficiency was partially a response to the rapid increases in crude oil prices in the 1970s.

Renewable Energy Sources

RECENT TRENDS: In the 1970s, the federal government's renewable energy program grew rapidly to include not only basic and applied **research and development (R & D)**, but also participation in private sector initiatives. In the 1980s, this interest waned as the price of oil fell. Government spending for R&D in renewable energy declined from a peak of $823 million in 1981 to a low of $139 million in 1990. Since 1990, this trend has reversed, largely due to concerns about petroleum supplies and environmental damage, especially acid rain and global warming, from burning fossil fuels.

To what extent the United States continues to subsidize the development of renewable energy will be a subject of much future debate.

RENEWABLE ENERGY SOURCES: The following information presents basic facts about five renewable energy sources and lists some advantages and disadvantages of each.

Solar Energy: **Solar energy** is produced in the core of the sun. In a process called **nuclear fusion**, the intense heat in the sun causes hydrogen atoms to break apart and fuse together to

form helium atoms. A very small amount of mass is lost in this process. This lost matter is emitted into space as radiant energy. Less than one percent of this energy reaches the earth, yet it is enough to provide all of the earth's energy needs. The sun's energy travels at the speed of light (186,000 miles per second) and reaches the earth in about eight minutes. Capturing the sun's energy is not easy since solar energy is spread out over such a large area. The energy a specific land area receives depends on various factors, such as time of day, season of the year, cloudiness of the sky, and proximity to the equator.

One primary use of solar energy is **home heating**. There are two basic kinds of solar heating systems: active and passive. In an **active system**, special equipment (such as a solar collector) is used to collect and distribute the solar energy. In a **passive system**, the home is designed to let in large amounts of sunlight. The heat produced from the light is trapped inside. A passive system does not rely on special mechanical equipment.

Another primary use of solar energy is **producing electricity**. The most familiar way is using **photovoltaic (PV) cells**, which are used to power toys, calculators, and roadside telephone call boxes. Photovoltaics is a process that directly converts solar energy to electricity. It has become more affordable due to private research. In 1976, the average market price for a photovoltaic module was $44 per peak watt installed, but by 2000 this had fallen to $3.46 per peak watt. The other primary way to produce electricity is using **solar thermal systems.** Large collectors concentrate the sunlight onto a receiver to superheat a liquid, which is used to make steam to power electrical generators.

Advantages of Solar Energy	Disadvantages of Solar Energy
* Unlimited supply	* May not be cost effective
* No air or water pollution	* Storage and backup are necessary
* High fixed, low operating costs reduce price volatility	* Reliability depends on availability of sunlight
	* Land intensive

Hydropower: **Hydropower** is energy that comes from the force of moving water. Hydropower is a renewable energy source because it is replenished constantly by the fall and flow of snow and rainfall in the **water cycle.** As water flows through devices such as a water wheel or turbine of a dam, the **kinetic** (motion) **energy** of water is converted to **mechanical energy**, which can be used to grind grain, drive a sawmill, pump water, or produce electricity.

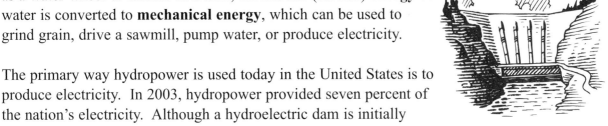

The primary way hydropower is used today in the United States is to produce electricity. In 2003, hydropower provided seven percent of the nation's electricity. Although a hydroelectric dam is initially expensive to build, in the long run, it is the cheapest way to produce electricity, primarily because the energy source, moving water, is free. Recently, some people have built smaller hydroelectric systems that produce enough electricity to power a few homes.

Advantages of Hydropower	Disadvantages of Hydropower
* Abundant, clean, and safe	* Significant environmental impact
* Easily stored in reservoirs	* Water supply is needed
* Relatively inexpensive way to produce electricity in the long run	* Best sites for dams already developed
* Recreational benefits like boating, fishing, etc.	

Wind Energy: **Wind** is air in motion. It is caused by the uneven heating of the earth's surface by the sun. Wind power has been used for thousands of years to convert the wind's kinetic (motion) energy into mechanical energy for grinding grain or pumping water. Today, wind machines are used increasingly to produce electricity.

The two most common types of wind machines used for producing electricity are horizontal and vertical. **Horizontal machines** have blades that look like airplane propellers. **Vertical machines** look like giant egg-beaters. The vertical machines are easier to maintain, can accept wind from any direction, and don't require protective features to guard against high winds. However, horizontal machines produce *more* electricity, and for this reason are used more than their vertical counterparts.

Most electricity production occurs on large **wind farms**. Most wind farms are owned by independent producers who operate the farms and sell electricity to utility companies for distribution. The **Public Utility Regulatory Policies Act (PURPA)** requires utility companies to purchase electricity from independent energy producers at fair and nondiscriminatory rates. In 2003, wind energy provided the United States with less than one percent of its total electricity. California currently produces twice as much as any other state. Many predict that wind energy will provide much more of our future electrical production.

Advantages of Wind Energy	Disadvantages of Wind Energy
* A "free" source of energy * No water or air pollution * Wind farms are relatively inexpensive to build. * High fixed, low operating costs reduce price volatility	* Requires constant and significant amounts of wind * Wind farms require large tracts of land. * Can have a negative visual impact on landscapes * Risk to endangered birds of prey

Geothermal Energy: **Geothermal energy** comes from the intense heat within the earth. The heat is produced by the radioactive decay of elements below the earth's surface. There is more than one kind of geothermal energy, but the only kind that is widely used is **hydrothermal energy**. Hydrothermal energy has two basic ingredients: water and heat. Water beneath the earth's surface contacts the heated rocks and changes into steam. Depending on the steam's temperature, it can heat buildings directly or can power turbines to generate electricity.

Using geothermal energy to produce electricity is a new industry in the United States. In a typical geothermal electric plant, steam is piped directly to a turbine which then powers an electrical generator. A geothermal wall can be one to two miles deep! In 1990, hydrothermal energy produced less than 0.5 percent of the electricity in the United States.

Advantages of Geothermal Energy	Disadvantages of Geothermal Energy
* Provides an unlimited supply of energy * Produces no air or water pollution	* Start-up/development costs can be expensive. * Maintenance costs, due to corrosion, can be a problem.

Biomass: **Biomass** is any organic substance that can be used as an energy source. The most common examples are wood, crops, seaweed, and animal wastes. Biomass has been used for thousands of years and is the oldest known energy source. It is a renewable energy source because its supply is unlimited – more can always be produced in a relatively short time.

All biomass is converted solar energy. The energy is stored in biomass through the process of **photosynthesis**, in which plants combine carbon dioxide, water, and certain minerals to form carbohydrates. The most common way to release the energy from biomass is burning. Other ways are bacterial decay, fermentation, and conversion.

There are four main types of biomass: 1. wood and agricultural products, 2. solid waste, 3. landfill gas, and 4. alcohol fuels. Wood is by far the most common form, accounting for about 70 percent of all biomass energy. Burning solid waste is a common practice, and people have done it for thousands of years. What is new is burning waste to produce electricity. **Waste-to-energy** power plants operate like a traditional coal plant, except garbage is used to produce steam to run the turbines. Although it typically costs more to produce electricity using biomass, the great advantage is that it reduces the

amount of waste entering landfills. Some people have environmental concerns about waste-to-energy plants, but because it is becoming increasingly difficult to determine sites for landfills, these plants are an increasingly attractive option.

The **methane** produced in landfills by the decay of organic matter is another source of biomass energy. A landfill owner in Indianapolis uses the methane to heat his greenhouse, thus reducing the operating costs of his on-site nursery business.

Corn, wheat, and other crops can be used to produce a variety of liquid fuels. The most common are ethanol and methanol. Today these are relatively high cost fuels, and the price of oil must continue to rise to make them a cost-effective option. However, a mixture of 10 percent ethanol and 90 percent gasoline produces a fuel called **gasohol**. Gasohol is more cost competitive and can be used in a traditional gasoline engine. It also has a higher octane rating than gasoline and is cleaner burning.

Advantages of Biomass	Disadvantages of Biomass
* Abundant and renewable	* Air pollution from burning biomass
* Way to dispose solid waste	* May not be cost-effective

Economic Implications

Energy policies have many economic implications. Two somewhat controversial issues concern the distinction between **energy efficiency** and **economic efficiency**, and the role of **market prices** in guiding decisions about energy resources.

ENERGY EFFICIENCY VERSUS ECONOMIC EFFICIENCY: Economists are concerned with the overall **economic efficiency** of the economic system. This means getting the greatest benefit from *all* of our **scarce** productive resources. **Energy efficiency**, a narrower concept, means getting the greatest benefit from our *energy* resources. Sometimes these goals conflict. For example, we could make automobiles today that average more than 100 miles per gallon. This would result in better **energy conservation**, but would we be willing to pay the cost in terms of lack of power, crash protection, and load capacity?

THE ROLE OF PRICE IN GUIDING DECISIONS ABOUT ENERGY: In market economies, resource allocation is guided primarily by market prices. These prices help society determine answers to the crucial questions of what, how, and for whom to produce. However, in the area of energy policy, many advocate significant levels of government intervention in energy markets. The intervention often takes the form of **subsidies** for the development of alternative energy sources which currently may not be cost-effective.

From 1995-2005, the **market price** of oil ranged from $22-50 per barrel. These prices are high enough for oil producers to make a profit and consumers to enjoy many benefits from this valuable source of energy. With colder winters and warmer summers, several devastating hurricanes, and the Iraq War, increased oil prices sparked higher gasoline prices during 2004-2005. In the future, these prices could possibly go even higher or could fall back to lower levels. Much depends on geopolitical events, since oil supplies are currently located in unstable regions. Oil remains an abundant source of energy. *Should the government subsidize more expensive forms of renewable energy, given the current price of oil (and other fossil fuels)?*

Proponents contend that subsidies are necessary to help reduce our dependence on finite fossil fuels. Proponents also point out that relying more on renewable energy will reduce our dependence on foreign oil suppliers and will result in less pollution of the environment.

 Subsidy opponents argue that we will never "run out" of fossil fuels. As fossil fuels become more scarce, their market price will rise, encouraging consumers to use less. The higher price also will make it profitable for energy companies to invest in new fossil fuel production technologies and in alternative energy sources, including renewable energy. This dynamic market product occurs automatically, without costly and inefficient government intervention. Opponents of subsidies would largely agree with subsidy proponents that the environmental costs of fossil fuels should be reflected in their price, which should be an important consideration when dealing with this issue. Opponents contend that the best way to lessen the danger of a cut-off in foreign supplies is for the U.S. government to build a **strategic petroleum reserve.**

The issue of the development of alternative energy sources is a complicated one. The key point to remember is that there is an **opportunity cost** to every economic decision. Using tax revenues to subsidize alternative energy means giving up some other valuable use for those revenues. In energy policy, as in all public policy, decision-makers must carefully consider the opportunity costs of different policy options.

Renewable Energy Vocabulary

BTU
British thermal unit; the amount of energy needed to raise the temperature of one pound of water one degree Fahrenheit

Economic Efficiency
Getting the most benefit from *all* of our scarce productive resources

Energy
The capacity to do work

Energy Conservation
Actions taken to get the most benefit from our scarce energy resources; promotes energy efficiency

Energy Efficiency
The amount of energy it takes to do a certain amount of work

Ethanol
A liquid, biomass fuel derived from crops, such as corn and wheat; ethyl alcohol

Gasohol
Biomass fuel produced by mixing ethanol and gasoline, typically 10 percent and 90 percent respectively

Geothermal Energy
Energy that comes from the heat within the earth

Hydropower
Energy that comes from the force of moving water

Hydrothermal Energy
Most common type of geothermal energy; consists of reservoirs of steam and/or hot water

Market Price
Price of a good, service, or energy resource, as determined by supply and demand in the marketplace

Methane
Colorless, odorless gas formed from the decay of an organic substance; identical to natural gas

Methanol
A liquid, alcohol fuel derived from wood, agricultural wastes, coal, and natural gas; methyl alcohol

Nonrenewable Energy
Energy resources, such as fossil fuels, that are limited in supply

OPEC
Organization of Petroleum Exporting Countries, a cartel that controls a significant part of the world's oil reserves

Opportunity Cost
The value of the best alternative when making a decision; every decision has an opportunity cost.

Photosynthesis
Process shared by all green plants by which solar energy is converted to chemical energy. Combines carbon dioxide, water, and various minerals to form carbohydrates

Primary Energy Source	Direct energy sources such as coal, oil, uranium, solar, and hydropower
Profit	The amount of sales revenue remaining after subtracting all the costs of production
PURPA	Public Utility Regulatory Policies Act; requires utility companies to purchase electricity from independent energy producers at fair and nondiscriminatory rates
Quad	One quadrillion (1,000,000,000,000,000) Btu's
Renewable Energy	Energy resources that are "unlimited" in supply because they can be replenished
Scarcity	In economics, the situation that exists whenever wants are greater than the resources available to satisfy the wants; scarcity requires people to make choices.
Secondary Energy Source	An energy source, such as electricity, that is produced using a primary energy source.
Solar Energy	Energy that comes from the sun
Subsidy	Financial assistance given by government to encourage the production of a good, service, or resource; production could be uneconomical without the subsidy.
Waste-to-Energy Plant	A facility that burns solid waste to produce usable energy
Wind Energy	Energy that comes from the movement of air

Teaching Instructions

Overview

These specific teaching activities, like those in the other units, do not have to be done in order. It may be best, however, to do the Case Study toward the end of the unit after students have mastered much of the basic information. Although some basic information is given in the Facts About Renewable Energy section, your students will need to research other resources to investigate the broad area of renewable energy adequately. The Resources section on page 157 identifies a variety of excellent sources. The Further Investigations activity suggests a variety of research activities.

Some of the key economic concepts in this unit are described below in the Important Concepts To Emphasize and Facts About Renewable Energy sections. Teachers may also wish to review the basic economic concepts relating to energy and the environment explained in the Introduction of this curriculum.

Important Concepts To Emphasize

1. A **subsidy** can take various forms, such as cash gifts, special tax credits to reduce tax liability below that of others in similar circumstances, or transfer of tangible or intangible property. Subsidies are not always stated explicitly in dollars. They can be hidden and hard to measure in money terms. A subsidy exists whenever one person or group receives something of value from another person or group without charge or expectation of compensation. For example, a government may give an income tax credit for homeowners who take certain actions to increase the energy efficiency of their homes or who use renewable energy sources to reduce their dependence on fossil fuels.

2. **There are no free sources of energy.** Everything has an opportunity cost. Even sources such as wind and solar power, which are readily available, cannot be developed without diverting resources from other social priorities.

3. **Conservation means more than just not using our natural resources.** One way of conserving energy resources is by using them efficiently. For example, we want to conserve petroleum so that we get the maximum benefit from our finite supplies; however, if we *never* use it, it has no value to us. We should manage our scarce natural resources to provide the greatest net benefit to present and future generations combined after considering all of the costs and benefits involved, including the environmental costs.

4. **As long as market prices are used to allocate energy resources, we will never run out of petroleum and other nonrenewable resources.** This is not to say that we can continue to use these energy sources without thought for tomorrow. Rather, it means that as an energy source becomes increasingly scarce, its market price will rise, discouraging consumption and encouraging production of alternative energy sources. During the 19th century, whalers nearly drove some species of whales to extinction. As this happened, the market price of whales and whale products inevitably rose. Eventually, whale oil became so expensive that petroleum became commercially feasible

as an energy source and whale oil lamps were phased out in favor of cheaper kerosene. The whales were actually saved by the free market response to their increasing scarcity.

5. **When people do not bear all of the costs of their actions, their decisions tend to be socially inefficient.** We implicitly subsidize fossil fuels whenever producers and consumers do not pay the full environmental costs of their actions. For example, without environmental regulations, consumers in Indiana would not pay the full social cost of producing electricity. To the extent that fossil fuel-burning power plants in the Midwest may contribute to acid rain in the northeast, consumers in Indiana receive a subsidy from the northeast by not paying the full environmental costs of their electricity. The economic reasons for restricting the use of high-sulphur coal is that producers and consumers who can shift the environmental damage to others have no incentive through the free market to use more expensive low-sulfer coal to generate power. Most of the benefits of using low-sulfur coal would go to other regions (the northeast and Canada), while the costs would be borne by Midwesterners. Restricting the use of high-sulphur coal would also have a very detrimental impact on the economics of states like Indiana, which have important coal-mining industries.

Teaching Suggestions

ACTIVITY 1: RENEWABLE ENERGY BASICS. Have the students research the renewable sources and complete the chart. Discuss the advantages and disadvantages of each.

ACTIVITY 2: GRAPHING ENERGY FACTS. In Part A and Part B, make sure students do an accurate job estimating the particular parts of the pie graphs. This involves correctly estimating angles of a circle. Also insist on graphs that are neatly drawn and labeled. You may want students to construct larger graphs for a bulletin board display.

ACTIVITY 3: TRENDS IN RESEARCH AND DEVELOPMENT (R & D) SPENDING. This activity shows the correlation between R & D funding appropriations and nominal oil prices. In question one, explain that to make accurate year-to-year comparisons of R & D spending, we should use **constant dollars** from a particular **base year.** If not, comparisons are distorted due to inflation.

In question 2, oil prices are quoted in **current year dollars.** Using **constant dollars** would give a truer picture of the *real* (inflation adjusted) changes in oil prices. Have some of your students determine the constant dollar prices of these oil prices. To do this they must use the **implicit price deflator (IPD)**, an index number used by economists to figure constant dollar (real) price changes. The IPD for each year since 1973 is given below, using 2000 as the **base year** (IPD = 100). To determine the real constant dollar price of oil for any year, use this formula:

$$\textbf{Constant Dollar Price} = (\textbf{Current Price/IPD}) \text{ x } 100$$

For example, in 1973 the current dollar price was $5 a barrel. The **constant dollar (real) price** is ($5/31.0) x 100 = $16.13. In other words, the $5 price in 1973 is equivalent to $16.13 using 2000 dollars. Have students figure and graph the *real* oil prices. Discuss how this graph differs from the graph of current dollar prices.

Implicit Price Deflators (1973 – 2005)									
1973	31.0	1980	52.2	1987	72.5	1994	89.6	2001	101.5
1974	33.4	1981	57.5	1988	74.6	1995	91.5	2002	103.6
1975	37.0	1982	61.5	1989	77.6	1996	94.5	2003	105.7
1976	39.4	1983	64.4	1990	80.4	1997	95.1	2004	108.0
1977	43.8	1984	66.8	1991	83.6	1998	96.1	2005	110.9
1978	44.5	1985	69.1	1992	87.0	1999	97.3		
1979	47.9	1986	70.6	1993	87.7	2000	100.0		

ACTIVITY 4: ENERGY EFFICIENCY. In question 4c, discuss why it is important to use **real (constant dollar) GDP** when analyzing changes in energy efficiency. (Answer: One should consider *actual* increases in the overall quantity of goods and services produced, not increases that result from the effects of inflation on the measured market value of goods and services.)

ACTIVITY 5: FURTHER INVESTIGATIONS. Encourage students to do research on their own. If time permits, let students share information they have learned with their classmates.

ACTIVITY 6: DEBATING THE ISSUES. Students can debate orally or present their views as a written assignment.

ACTIVITY 7: EEE ACTIONS. Encourage students to implement some of the suggested activities.

ACTIVITY 8: CASE STUDY: THE CASE OF THE RENEWABLE RESOURCES

This case study deals with a hypothetical congressional debate over an energy bill that would provide federal support to energy firms willing to increase their R & D spending for renewable energy sources such as solar, wind, biomass, and hydropower. The case uses role playing to encourage students to look at the trade-offs involved in energy policy and to recognize the role of values and self-interest in determining the appropriate public policy. Suggested steps to implement the case study are as follows:

1. Ask all the students to read background materials on energy. Assign half of the students to serve as senators who will listen to testimony and then vote on the bill to give tax breaks to developers of renewable energy sources. The other half of the class should be divided into small groups representing some or all of the following groups: 1. fossil fuel producers and consumers, 2. developers of solar, wind, and geothermal power, 3. environmental groups, and 4. consumers in areas such as New

England, which has good potential for hydropower, but depends on Midwestern coal and OPEC petroleum.

2. Each special interest group should fill out a Decision Worksheet and Decision Grid reflecting its perspective on the problem. Each group should then elect a spokesperson to provide testimony in the Senate hearings.

3. After hearing from the affected groups, members of the Senate should develop a consensus decision worksheet and vote on the energy bill.

4. In a debriefing session, ask students to defend their positions as either special interest groups or Senators voting on the issue.

Key Questions To Ask Students

1. What is a subsidy? *(financial assistance provided by a person or group to another person or group in the form of cash, tax breaks, or the transfer of something of value without payment)*

2. What is a tax credit? *(a tax break or rebate in the form of a special reduction in taxes that otherwise would have been due by an individual taxpayer or class of taxpayers)*

3. Why are there no "free" sources of energy? *(Nothing is free in the sense that everything has an opportunity cost, represented by the best alternative that was given up in making a choice.)*

4. Why should solar energy companies care that fossil fuels can damage the environment? *(Solar companies feel that getting use of the environment for free represents a subsidy for fossil fuels that lowers their price below the full social cost, making it hard for nonpolluting energy sources to compete.)*

5. What is the difference between a renewable and a nonrenewable energy resource? *(Unlike renewable energy resources such as sunlight, water power, and wind, nonrenewable energy resources exist in finite quantities that cannot be replaced when they are used up.)*

6. If petroleum is a nonrenewable resource, how can it be that we will never run out? *(As oil gets harder to extract from increasingly less productive deposits, the price will rise. Consumers and producers will have the incentive to find cheaper alternatives and producers will have the incentive to find more oil.)*

Unit 3

Renewable Energy Resources

Student Activities

Activity 1

Renewable Energy Basics

1. Complete the chart below about the basic types of **renewable energy** resources.

Type	Definition	Examples	Advantages	Disadvantages
Solar				
Hydropower				
Wind Energy				
Geothermal				
Biomass				

2. List energy sources that are **fossil fuels**. _____

_____

3. What main *advantage* do fossil fuels have over renewable energy resources?

_____

_____

4. What are two *disadvantages* of fossil fuels compared to renewable energy resources?

_____

_____

Activity 2

Graphing Energy Facts

PART A: The table below lists United States primary energy consumption by source in 1973, 1991, and 2005.

Primary Energy Consumption (percent)			
	1973	**1991**	**2005**
Petroleum	46.9	40.4	37.2
Nuclear Power	1.2	8.0	8.3
Hydropower/Other Renewable	4.1	4.0	8.0
Natural Gas	30.3	24.4	23.7
Coal	17.5	23.2	22.8

1. Draw three pie graphs showing these data. Use different colors to identify each energy source and neatly label your graphs. Then answer the questions that follow.

2. What is a **primary** energy source? Explain how it differs from a **secondary** source.
    _____
    _____
    _____

3. Which source *decreased* the most between 1973 and 2005? _____

    Why do you think these decreases occurred? _____
    _____
    _____
    _____

4. Which source *increased* the most between 1973 and 2005? _____

    Why do you think this happened? _____
    _____
    _____

5. Sunlight, wind, and running water are essentially "free." Yet renewable energy sources are a very small part of our energy consumption. Why is this? Explain. _____

_____

_____

_____

PART B: The data below show the amount of electricity generated in the United States in 2002 by various renewable energy sources. Compute percent of total.

2002 United States Renewable Electricity Net Generation (Gigawatts)		
		Percent of Total
Geothermal	14.5	
Hydroelectric	264.3	
Biomass (Municipal Waste and Landfill Gas)	20.2	
Biomass (other)	2.7	
Solar Thermal	.6	
Wind	10.4	
Wood/Wood Waste	38.7	
TOTAL RENEWABLE	351.4	

Source: http://www.eia.doe.gov/cneaf/solar.renewables/page/rea_data/tableb2.html

1. Draw a bar graph illustrating renewable generating capacity. On the vertical axis put Electrical Generating/Gigawatts. On the horizontal axis put the Energy Sources. Use different colors and neatly label your graph. Also, give the graph a title.

2. Compute the percent of the total that each resource provides and put the percent in the blanks. Then make a pie graph of the percent data. Use different colors and neatly label the graph. Also, give your graph a title.

3. Which renewable source is used the most for producing electricity? _____

    Why? _____

    _____

    _____

4. Which renewable energy source above is used the least? _____

5. Which renewable source do you think *should* be used the most? Why? _____

    _____

    _____

    _____

Activity 3

Trends In R & D Funding

1. The United States Department of Energy (DOE) **subsidizes** research and development (R&D) in renewable energy. The data below show R & D funding since 1981 in current (nominal) dollars. The FY stands for fiscal year. Construct a line graph showing R & D funding by year. (Put R&D funding on the vertical axis and Fiscal Year on the horizontal axis.)

DOE Renewable Energy R & D Funding ($$'s in millions - Congressional Appropriations)							
FY 1981	823	FY 1988	146	FY 1995	373	FY 2002	385
FY 1982	401	FY 1989	148	FY 1996	284	FY 2003	322
FY 1983	304	FY 1990	139	FY 1997	266	FY 2004	357
FY 1984	256	FY 1991	198	FY 1998	294	FY 2005	475
FY 1985	240	FY 1992	240	FY 1999	332	FY 2006	487
FY 1986	199	FY 1993	256	FY 2000	308		
FY 1987	172	FY 1994	324	FY 2001	370		

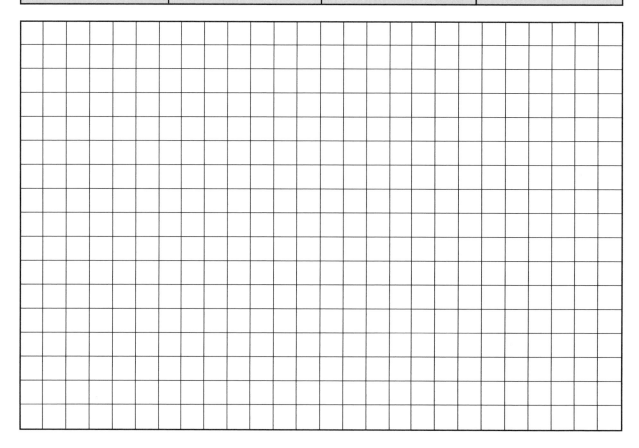

2. Describe trends in R & D funding that you observe. How does inflation affect your conclusions?

_____

_____

3. The data below give the average **current dollar (nominal)** price per barrel of oil since 1973. Price is rounded to the nearest dollar. Construct a line graph showing the data. (Put "Price" on the vertical axis and "Year" on the horizontal axis.)

Average Price of Oil (current dollars)					
1973	$5	1984	$29	1995	$17
1974	$9	1985	$27	1996	$20
1975	$12	1986	$14	1997	$19
1976	$13	1987	$18	1998	$12
1977	$14	1988	$15	1999	$17
1978	$15	1989	$18	2000	$27
1979	$25	1990	$23	2001	$23
1980	$37	1991	$20	2002	$23
1981	$36	1992	$19	2003	$28
1982	$32	1993	$17	2004	$38
1983	$29	1994	$16	2005	$50

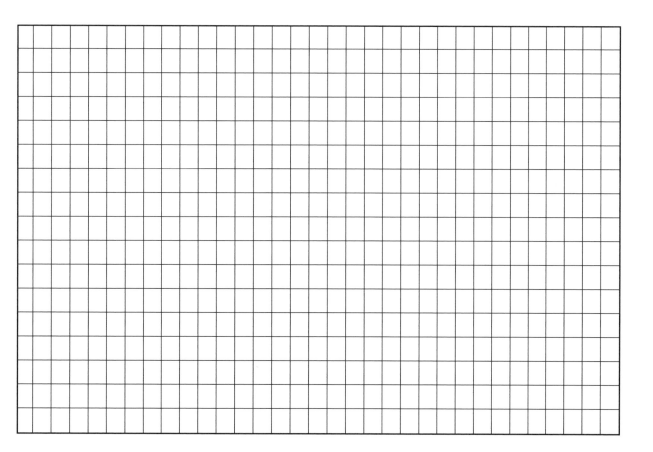

4. Describe oil price trends. Do they help explain the trends you observe in R&D funding?

_____

_____

_____

Activity 4

Energy Efficiency

1. Define **energy efficiency.** _____

2. List four ways you can be more energy efficient at *home*? _____

    _____

3. What are ways that a *business* can be more energy efficient? _____

    _____

4. The graph and chart below show total United States energy consumption from 1973 to 2004.

United States Energy Consumption (Trillion Btu's)			
1973	75,708	1990	84,704
1974	73,991	1991	84,643
1975	71,999	1992	85,992
1976	76,012	1993	87,619
1977	78,000	1994	89,283
1978	79,986	1995	91,250
1979	80,903	1996	94,256
1980	78,289	1997	94,769
1981	76,342	1998	95,192
1982	73,253	1999	96,836
1983	73,101	2000	98,961
1984	76,736	2001	96,472
1985	76,469	2002	97,877
1986	76,782	2003	98,311
1987	79,225	2004	99,740
1988	82,844		
1989	84,957		

a. What was the increase in consumption from 1973 to 2004? _____

b. Compute the *percentage* increase from 1973 to 2004. (Use 1973 as the base year.) ____

c. The Gross Domestic Product (GDP) measures the market value of all final goods and services produced in an economy in a year. Since 1973, the **real GDP** (expressed in year 2000 dollars) of the United States has increased 148 percent. Given this fact and your answer in b. above, what can you conclude about the **energy efficiency** of the United States from 1973 to 2004?

    _____

    _____

    _____

5. The United States consumes more energy per unit of GDP than Japan or Italy. (2005: U.S. 8.02 thousand Btu's, Japan 5.85, Italy 4.95) Give at least two reasons for this difference.

    _____

    _____

Activity 5

Further Investigations

1. Research the history of **solar energy**. How did people in earlier times harness this form of energy? What developments have taken place in the past 100 years? Prepare a report of your findings. Include diagrams and pictures of various solar energy systems.

2. Prepare a report on **passive** and **active** solar heating systems. Include diagrams or pictures in your report. Find out the cost difference between the two systems. If possible, visit a home that uses solar heating. Interview the owner to identify advantages and disadvantages of the solar system.

3. Research how a solar **thermal power plant** produces electricity. Diagram how such a system works. What are the kilowatt hour costs of producing electricity using this method? What does the future hold for these types of power plants?

4. Research developments in **solar-powered cars.** What are the advantages and disadvantages of these vehicles? What does the future hold for solar-powered transportation?

5. Research another new form of solar thermal power: the **solar pond.** Describe and diagram how it works. Explain what promise this type of solar power holds for the future.

6. Investigate developments in **photovoltaic** solar power technology.

7. Research the history of **wind energy**. Investigate how people in earlier times and in different cultures have harnessed the wind's energy. What developments have taken place in the past hundred years? How is wind energy being used today? Include diagrams and pictures in your report.

8. Prepare a report on how electricity is generated on **wind farms**. Describe types of wind generators, types and sizes of wind farms, the economics of electricity production on wind farms, and the locations of currently operating wind farms in the United States. Include diagrams.

9. **The Public Utility Regulatory Policies Act (PURPA)** of 1978 requires utilities to buy electricity at reasonable rates from independent electricity producers. Research other specific requirements of the law. Contact your local electrical utility company and find out how PURPA has affected its operation.

10. Explain and diagram how a **hydroelectric** power plant operates. Label your diagram carefully. Identify some of the environmental concerns about constructing this type of power plant. Research the kilowatt hour (kWh) cost of electricity produced in these plants. How does the cost compare with electrical production using other forms of energy?

11. Research how **tidal power** and **ocean thermal energy conversion** can be used to generate electricity.

12. Diagram and explain the operation of a **waste-to-energy** power plant. If possible, visit a plant in operation. The COVANTA facility in Indianapolis provides teachers with information and also schedules free tours.

13. Research these four basic methods of capturing geothermal energy: **dry steam** systems, **wet steam** systems, **geopressurized hot water** systems, and **hot dry-rock** systems.

14. Research how **geothermal** energy can be used to heat homes. Diagram how such a geothermal system works. Investigate the costs compared to other types of home heating systems.

15. Research current developments in alternative fuels, especially **ethanol, methanol,** and **gasohol.** How are they made? What are the advantages and disadvantages of each type of fuel? What states lead in the production and consumption of these fuels?

16. Research the advantages and disadvantages of using **wood** as a fuel. Be sure to examine how wood is used for fuel in other countries of the world.

17. Investigate the topic of **superconductivity.** Find out how this development has the potential to change, or even revolutionize, the electronic, electric power, and transportation industries.

18. As you study energy, put information on a timeline made of paper. Stretch the timeline across one wall. Mark important discoveries, inventors, and places related to energy.

19. Plan a trip to a local power plant. Prepare questions beforehand to ask plant officials. Prepare a report of your visit, including diagrams of the energy production process.

20. Assign a research paper in which students address how the United States should react to a severe energy crisis. Identify what policies should be encouraged and/or avoided.

21. Research nuclear energy in the United States. What are the trends in investment in nuclear energy? What are the advantages and disadvantages of nuclear energy?

Activity 6

Debating the Issues

Debate and discuss these statements:

1. To help lessen our dependence on foreign energy, especially oil, the United States should *increase* funding for renewable energy substantially, even though this will *reduce* funding for other important programs.

2. United States car companies should be *required* to produce a solar-powered car since this will help reduce our consumption of polluting fossil fuels.

3. The government should quit subsidizing R & D in renewable energy. When the price of nonrenewable sources becomes high enough it will then be profitable for private energy firms to invest in renewable energy technology. Until then, money currently spent on R & D should be used for more urgent needs, such as cancer research, toxic waste clean-up, and better roads.

4. To lessen our dependence on foreign oil and to spur development in alternative energy sources, including renewable energy, the United States should impose an additional gasoline tax of $1 per gallon.

5. To reduce the consumption of fossil fuels, we should develop hydropower as much as possible. We should build more dams and reservoirs, even if it means disrupting to a degree the ecological balance of certain rivers and streams. Reservoirs also provide many valuable recreational benefits.

6. We should encourage communities to develop environmentally safe waste-to-energy power plants. Not only does this reduce what is put into our landfills, but it also uses our solid waste to produce energy.

Activity 7

EEE Actions:
You Can Make A Difference!

1. Do an energy audit in your home. Check ways to make your home more energy efficient. Make energy saving changes if possible, such as improving insulation, installing storm doors and windows, stopping drafts under doors and around windows, and installing devices that reduce hot water consumption.

2. Plant shade trees around your house. This will make your house cooler and lessen the need for air conditioning.

3. Investigate the feasibility of installing a solar heating system in your house.

4. Recycle where feasible. Recycling certain items such as aluminum cans can save enormous amounts of energy. Try to buy recycled products and products that use minimum packaging.

5. Use your appliances efficiently. For example, run dishwashers and washing machines when you have full loads, wash clothes in cold water, don't overheat your hot water, use a clothes line instead of the dryer, and buy energy efficient appliances.

6. Dress for the season! In the winter, wear warm clothes inside your house and turn down the thermostat a bit! In the summer, wear cool, loose clothes. Try not to turn on air conditioning until it gets really hot.

7. If feasible, walk or ride a bike to school or around town. It's good exercise and it saves energy!

8. Ask your principal if your school has a plan for reducing energy consumption. If not, ask if your class can conduct an energy audit. Discuss possible improvements and draft a letter with suggestions for reducing your school's energy consumption.

9. Design energy conservation awareness posters and place them in the hallways at school.

10. Be sure that your family car has a regular tune-up. Keep the tires inflated properly.

Activity 8

Case Study

The Case of the Energy Subsidy

Student Directions:

1. The Senate is considering energy policies to give tax breaks to renewable energy sources and to increase taxes on fossil fuels. You will be asked to take part in public hearings involving these issues.

2. After you research the various energy sources, you will be assigned a role as either a senator or one of the lobbyists representing various special interests and geographic regions.

3. Fill out a Decision Worksheet and Decision-Making Grid to help you come to a decision. Much depends on you!

SCENARIO

The year is 2006. United States dependence on foreign petroleum, which became a problem in the 1970s, continues to grow. In addition, there is a rising concern over environmental costs associated with the use of fossil fuels. Renewable energy sources are an option in some regions, but they have been slow to develop commercially. Connecticut, for example, has access to hydroelectric power, but usage has actually declined during the past century because of relatively cheap fossil fuels. To help change this trend, Connecticut Senator Jonathan Barnhart has sponsored a bill to provide special tax breaks for developers of renewable energy sources, including solar, wind, geothermal, hydropower, and biomass. These tax subsidies would take the form of tax credits (rebates) for qualifying energy projects.

Senator Barnhart's proposal received a mixed review in the Senate. Senators from the five top oil-producing states – Texas, Alaska, Louisiana, California, and Oklahoma - expressed concern that the bill would put oil producers at a disadvantage, resulting in serious job losses in their states. Three of those states, Texas, Louisiana, and Oklahoma, are also the top producers of natural gas, leading their senators to argue even more strongly against a subsidy for competing renewable fuels. Noting that renewable fuels are not yet competitive in price without tax subsidies, they argue that consumers would get the best product at the lowest price by letting the market determine what type of energy to produce and in what quantities. In addition, they object to any programs that would increase the size of the federal budget deficit at a time when program cuts and tax hikes are being proposed to deal with the out-of-control federal budget.

Environmental groups and developers of renewable energy sources disagree. They claim that fossil fuels already receive a subsidy from the general public in the form of environmental damage that does not get charged back to those who are responsible. They assert that fossil fuels would cost a lot more if the environmental costs to society were included. According to the environmentalists, we tend to be short-sighted in dealing with nonrenewable resources by not taking into account their finite nature until it is too late.

Oil company representatives respond that it was the free market that developed petroleum back in the mid-nineteenth century when whales became relatively scarce and there was concern they might be driven to extinction. Oklahoma Senator, Susan Phillips, reminded Senator Barnhart that we avoided whale oil crises a century ago not through special subsidies, but through the free market response to the rising price of whale oil. "The higher price of whale oil actually created a market for petroleum and other energy sources by encouraging both consumers and producers to look for cheaper alternatives."

The president of the Sierra Club, Belinda Arbuckle, disagreed. "For free markets to operate effectively, people need to pay the full cost of their actions. Our failure to take into account the full long-run costs of fossil fuels to society makes it difficult for producers of renewable energy sources to compete. I propose new taxes on fossil fuels reflecting the environmental damage associated with their production and use. This would increase the price of fossil fuels, reflecting their environmental impact and making it easier for renewable energy sources to compete on the basis of price."

The fossil fuel industry response is that we do not need another tax on energy to clean up the environment, especially in light of the mixed scientific evidence on the damaging effects of sulphur dioxide and other pollutants from fossil fuels. The industry also reminded the senators that an energy tax would have negative effects on jobs and growth throughout an economy dependent on fossil fuels.

The Senate is undecided about what to do and is calling for special hearings. Should the Senate, 1. support the Barnhart proposal to grant subsidies to producers of renewable energy, 2. support the Sierra Club proposal to tax fossil fuels, or 3. do neither and let free markets determine energy use?

Answers to Selected Teaching Activities

Activity 1: Renewable Energy Basics

1.   Definitions, examples, and specific advantages and disadvantages are listed in the Facts About Renewable Energy section.

2.   The primary fossil fuel energy sources are petroleum, natural gas, and coal.

3.   The main advantage of fossil fuels is that they are relatively abundant, and therefore, relatively inexpensive.

4.   The primary disadvantage of fossil fuels is that they are more polluting than renewable energy sources. The burning of fossil fuels also produces carbon dioxide, which some fear is causing global warming. This, however, is still only a theory, and has not been confirmed by scientific evidence. See Unit 4 on global warming.

Activity 2: Graphing Energy Facts

Part A:

1.   Make sure students have neatly labeled, colored graphs.

2.   Primary energy sources are basic sources of energy, such as coal, natural gas, hydropower, wind, petroleum, etc. Secondary sources such as electricity require primary sources of energy to generate power.

3.   Petroleum (46.9 percent to 37.2 percent). This large decrease occurred because the price of oil increased significantly in the 1970s. As price increased, oil consumers bought less, switched to substitutes, etc.

4.   Nuclear power. Nuclear power is clean and relatively cost-effective. While much of the increased capacity in nuclear power prior to the 1970s was already planned, the oil price increases certainly encouraged the increased use of nuclear power. However, the Three Mile Island incident in 1979 caused much public opposition to nuclear energy. The growth in the amount of nuclear-generated electrical power has tapered off in recent years and could possibly diminish in the near future as older power plants are retired. However, recent high oil prices are reviving an interest in nuclear power, which may reverse this trend. The future looks brighter for coal, although the current fear of global warming is causing second thoughts about relying more and more on coal.

5.   The major reason is that, compared to other sources of energy, renewable sources are relatively more expensive.

Part B:

1. Make sure student graphs are neatly labeled and use several colors.

2. Hydropower 85.9 percent, Geothermal 3.0 percent, Biomass (Municipal Waste to Energy) 2.3 percent, Biomass - Other (especially wood and wood waste) 6.7 percent, Solar Thermal 0.5 percent, Wind 1.6 percent.

3. Hydropower. It is relatively cost-effective compared to the other sources.

4. Solar thermal

5. Answers will vary.

Activity 3: Trends in R & D Funding

1. Make sure students label the axes correctly. You may have to help students determine the range of R & D on the vertical axis. A workable range is $0 to $900 millions.

2. R & D funding decreased in the 1980s, then began increasing again. Students should keep in mind that these are nominal, not constant, dollar figures.

3. Make sure students label the graph correctly and put a workable range of prices on the vertical axis ($0 to $50). You can have students graph the *real* price changes in oil, too, using 2000 dollars. See teacher directions for this activity.

4. Oil prices rose sharply in the 1970s, then plunged in the mid-1980s and 1990s. Since then prices have increased again, especially in 2003-2005. In this time period, R&D funding did rise, and can be expected to continue if oil prices remain high and if environmental concerns about burning fossil fuels continue.

Activity 4: Energy Efficiency

1. Energy efficiency measures the amount of energy it takes to do a certain amount of work or do a certain task.

2. Answers will vary. Examples: Add insulation, install energy efficient appliances, turn down the thermostat, run dishwashers and washing machines only when fully loaded.

3. Answers will vary. Examples: improved energy management such as better maintenance, improved insulation, conservation goals, controlling thermostats, routine energy audits, use of computers to monitor energy consumption, heat recovery and heat exchange, improvements in electricity cogeneration, investment in energy efficient production technologies.

4.   a. $99,740 - 75,708 = 24,032$ trillion Btu's b. $24,032/75,708 = 31.7$ percent
      c.   Energy efficiency has increased greatly.

5. "Energy efficiency" is a commonly used statistic to make comparisons among countries; however, it can be misleading since it does not take into account differences in life styles, population density, industry mix, and other factors. For example, Japan and Italy are small countries with high population densities. This makes energy-saving mass transit more practical. Italy and Japan also tax energy much more heavily (In Italy, gas currently costs close to $6 a gallon, of which about three-fourths is tax, which reduces energy consumption.) The United States has a more extreme climate, which requires large amounts of energy for heating and cooling. Living standards also are higher in the United States, and it takes more energy to heat our large homes. When corrected for differences in living space, the United States is among the most efficient of the other developed countries in residential heating. Another factor is that because energy is relatively abundant in the United States compared to in Japan and Italy, we have developed industries that rely on high energy usage ("energy intensity") in production.

Activity 8: Case Study: The Case of the Energy Subsidy

The Decision Worksheets for the various special interest groups will reflect the biases of the constituencies represented. Nevertheless, the consensus Decision Grid is likely to look something like the sample below.

Suggested Answer Key The Case of the Energy Subsidy					
Alternatives	**Criteria**				
	Fairness	**Environmental Impact**	**Deals with Spillover Costs**	**Growth and Jobs**	**Budget Deficit**
Free market only	− Pollution hurts others	− Benign neglect	− Does not deal with spillover	+ Growth continues	0 No direct impact
Tax credits	+/− Why single out this industry?	+ Encourages cleaner fuels	? Could level playing field with fossil fuels, but hard to measure	+ Growth continues	− Reduces tax revenues
Fossil fuel tax	+ Those responsible would pay	+ Incentive to develop cleaner fuels	+ Would internalize spillover costs	− Energy costs would rise, slowing the economy	+ Increases tax revenues

Unit 4

Global Warming

Overview of Unit 4

Global Warming

Introduction

In this unit students analyze the complex topic of global warming. Your students will discover that there remains some scientific uncertainty about global warming. This makes it challenging for public policy makers, who must decide whether or not to implement costly greenhouse gas reduction policies which may yield uncertain results far into the future.

Learning Objectives

<u>After completing this unit students will:</u>

1. Explain the greenhouse effect.
2. Explain why the issue of greenhouse warming involves spillover costs.
3. Identify advantages and disadvantages of a carbon tax.
4. Understand that public policy decisions involve trade-offs among goals.

Unit Outline

I.   Framing the Debate

II.   Facts about Global Warming

III.   Global Warming Vocabulary

IV.   Teaching Instructions and Key Questions To Emphasize

V.   Specific Teaching Activities
1. Greenhouse Warming: What Is It?
2. How Much Is Enough?
3. Analyzing Greenhouse Data
4. Further Investigations
5. Debating the Issues
6. EEE Actions – You Can Make A Difference!
7. Case Study

VI.   Answers to Selected Teaching Activities

Framing the Debate

The Pessimist View

With a photo of a polar bear stranded on a fractured ice floe, the feature story on the cover of *Time Magazine* (April 3, 2006) is titled:

> ### Special Report – Global Warming
>
> ### Be Worried. Be *Very* Worried.
>
> **Climate change isn't some vague future problem –
> It's already damaging the planet at an alarming pace.**

In 2004, *Science* surveyed 928 articles published in refereed scientific journals and found that "none of the papers disagreed with the consensus position" that global warming is a reality and that human activity is the primary cause. Also, some conservative evangelical ministers have recently challenged their congregations to address global warming.

The Optimist View

Sixty leading scientists signed an open letter to Canada's new Prime Minister, Stephen Harper, encouraging him to reconsider their nation's commitment to the Kyoto Protocol Agreement to reduce Greenhouse Gas Emissions (GHG) that supposedly cause global warming, according to the *Canadian Financial Post* (first week of April, 2006):

> **Climate change is a meaningless phrase used repeatedly by activists to convince the public that a climate catastrophe is looming and humanity is he cause. Neither of these fears is justified.**
>
> **Global climate changes all the time due to natural causes, and the human impact still remains impossible to distinguish from this natural 'noise.'**

Along the same lines, the George C. Marshall Institute has studied the issue for decades and recently published *Shattered Consensus: The True State of Global Warming* (Washington, DC: www.marshall.org), a collection of ten essays challenging the alleged consensus position. "The beauty of science is that truth is determined by observation and not by consensus. The seemly endless press releases, commentary, and resolutions claiming a consensus for the anthropogenic climate change hypothesis are scientifically meaningless."[1]

---

1. Comments on the content of *Shattered Consensus* by Dr. David Douglas, Professor of Physics, University of Rochester. See http://www.marshall.org/article.php?id=357.

Figure 1

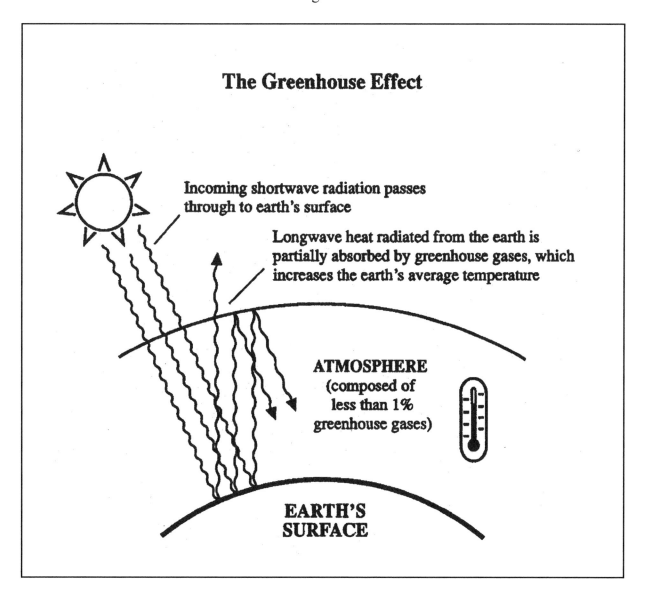

Entering the Debate

What is one to make of these polarized views? Students and all scholars must appeal to the facts as we know them. In the case of global warming, the facts are complex and somewhat uncertain.

Some Facts About Global Warming

Introduction

The topic of global warming is currently receiving world-wide attention. The United Nations established a clearinghouse, the U.N. Intergovernmental Panel on Climate Change (IPCC), for study and information. Despite the uncertainty surrounding this issue, global warming is a cause of concern for many scientists, policy-makers, and lay citizens. In the United States, the Bush administration has refused to sign the Kyoto Protocol, an international effort among 141 countries to reduce greenhouse gases (GHGs), on the grounds that it places an unfair burden on the U.S. economy to reduce industrial emissions. Some countries resent our rejection of Kyoto because, with only five percent of the world's population, the U.S. produces 25 percent of CO_2 emissions. Consequently, over 200 U.S. mayors signed the Mayors Climate Protection Agreement, pledging to meet the Kyoto standards on GHG emissions by 2012. In the Eastern U.S., nine states have established the Regional Greenhouse Gas Initiative to develop a cap-and-trade program among polluting companies. The following information provides some basic facts about global warming and clarifies some of the policy options for dealing with this environmental concern.

The "Greenhouse Effect"

The concern about global warming centers on a common scientific phenomenon known as the "greenhouse effect." This concept is rather simple. Certain GHGs in the earth's atmosphere let sunlight through to the earth's surface and then trap (absorb) outgoing infrared (long-wave) radiation in much the same way that a greenhouse prevents heat from escaping through its tinted panels. This greenhouse effect is beneficial to life on earth since, without this warming, the earth's average temperature would be about 63 degrees F (35 degrees C) cooler and would be much less suitable for human life.

The primary greenhouse gases are carbon dioxide (CO_2) and methane (CH_4). Water vapor also exhibits greenhouse gas characteristics and is often classified as a greenhouse gas. Chlorofluorocarbons (CFCs) and nitrous oxide (N_2O) are minor greenhouse gases, although some scientists believe that CFCs play a relatively significant role in greenhouse warming. Despite their contribution to the greenhouse effect, all the greenhouse gases make up less than 0.04 percent of the world's atmosphere, with carbon dioxide comprising about 0.03 percent.

All the greenhouses except CFCs occur *naturally* in the atmosphere. The amount of carbon that is cycling from naturally occurring processes in the biosphere as CO_2 is enormous – about 700 billion tons. Based on historical data, scientists believe that the general long-term climate stability indicates that the amounts of CO_2 generated by natural processes have, until recently, been about equal to the amounts absorbed by these processes. Methane is the major component of natural gas and is also produced by many biological processes. Naturally occurring nitrous oxide emissions come from biological processes in the soil.

Human activities affect the naturally occurring concentrations of the greenhouse gases. The burning of fossil fuels is the human activity that most affects the concentration of carbon dioxide. Methane comes from cattle-raising, rice paddies, and trash dumps, as well as from natural gas lost to the atmosphere during industrial production processes. Human-related increase in nitrous oxides comes mainly from fuel combustion. CFCs are stable, nontoxic compounds that contain carbon, chlorine, fluoride, and sometimes hydrogen. They have increased as a result of their use in refrigerants, cleaning solvents, aerosol propellants, and the manufacture of plastic foams. The

production of CFCs is leveling off largely due to the provisions of the 1987 Montreal Protocol on Substances that Deplete the Ozone Layer. Some current evidence indicates that the global warming effects of the CFCs may be less than scientists had previously thought.

The current controversy about global warming reflects fears about increasing concentrations of greenhouse gases, especially CO_2. Pessimistic scientists and environmentalists believe these increasing concentrations have intensified the greenhouse effect, causing average earth temperatures to rise. This could produce dire results, including crop failures, increased storm intensity, and coastal flooding resulting from rising sea levels. Other scientists, however, believe that these fears are exaggerated, and that there is little danger of catastrophic climate change. According to the optimistic view, policies to drastically reduce greenhouse gas emissions would be a mistake since these policies would have harmful effects on the world's economies. According to the U.S. National Oceanic and Atmospheric Administration, global surface temperatures have increased about $0.6^{\circ}C$ since the late 19th century and about $0.25^{\circ}C$ during the past 25 years (www.ncdc.noaa.gov/oa/climate/globalwarming.html). Geographically, the warming has not been globally uniform.

Does the Greenhouse Effect Cause Global Warming?

Many scientists are studying the greenhouse effect to determine if severe climate change is likely. There is general agreement that concentrations of greenhouse gases have and will continue to increase due largely to anthropogenic causes (human activity), especially the burning of fossil fuels. Scientists estimate that since the beginning of the Industrial Revolution (after 1750), concentrations of CO_2 have increased by 20 percent and CH_4 by more than 50 percent. Concentrations of CO_2 are rising by 0.5 percent per year and CH_4 by 0.9 percent per year. CFCs do not occur naturally and were not found in the atmosphere until a few decades ago.

During the last ice age, concentrations of CO_2 in the atmosphere dipped to 180 parts per million (ppm). Concentrations which rose to 280 ppm just prior to the modern age are now at 381 ppm

and are projected to rise to 450 ppm by the end of this century, which might increase global temperatures by six percent, according to the pessimistic view.

While there is agreement that greenhouse gas concentrations have increased, it is *not* possible at this time to tell whether this increase is causing global warming. Temperature readings around the world have been recorded consistently only during the past 100 years. During this time the average global temperature has risen about 0.5 degrees C, with most of this increase occurring between 1890 and 1940. However, 19 of the 20 hottest years on record have occurred since 1980. While some scientists believe this warming is due to increasing greenhouse emissions, other scientists point out that the temperature increase could also be attributed to natural climate variability. Given today's limited understanding of climate change, neither possibility can be ruled out completely.

Climate Feedback Loops

Climatology is complex because of potentially intricate feedback loops in nature. For example, polar ice reflects sunlight, but ocean water absorbs it, continually increasing water temperature relative to the ice caps, which means that each mile of melting ice dissipates faster than the previous miles.

Another example is Europe. Although it has the same latitude as Alaska, its climate is much warmer due to the Atlantic Gulf Stream, which brings warm water from the tropics north to Western Europe's shores, and then flows back south underneath the Gulf Stream currents because cold water is heavier than warm water. European civilization depends on this feedback phenomenon. However, when ice caps melt, releasing fresh water into the currents, their salinity drops, making the south-flowing submerged cold water lighter. It then surfaces and disrupts the Gulf Stream mechanism. The implications for Europe are significant, in the pessimistic view.

Measurement Models

Throughout the debates about global warming, one point of argument always arises: what year or time period or geologic era should be used as the basis for measuring change? Some pessimistic scientists who believe that greenhouse warming is a serious problem base their predictions primarily on complex, theoretical computer models known as General Circulation Models (GCMs) that rely on indirect estimates of ancient temperatures and CO_2 concentrations based on perceived changes in polar ice cap dimensions and chemical composition of deeply buried ice. A typical GCM involves hundreds of equations and dozens of variables. Scientists have developed several versions of GCMs. Some models focus on recent centuries as the base period. The global temperature change predictions of these models generally assume an increase of 40-60 percent over pre-industrial levels (280 ppm) of carbon dioxide some time in the middle of this century. We are currently at 381 ppm and rising. Current GCM simulations based on this assumption show a range of average global temperature increases of 3.4 degrees to 9.4 degrees F cumulatively since records have been kept. However, in its final report to Congress, the National Academy of Sciences concluded that because of the large degree of uncertainty associated with the GCMs, prudent public policy should be based on a possible global average temperature increase of between 1.8 degrees to 9.0 degrees F. The Academy concluded that, "It is still unreasonable to expect current GCMs to provide precise prediction, decades into the future, of global average temperature…Substantial improvements in GCM capabilities are needed for GCM forecasts to increase their credibility."[2]

More optimistic scientists tend to have less confidence in the predictive ability of the GCMs. They believe that more accurate predictions of the greenhouse effect can be made by analyzing actual temperature data from the last 100 years. According to these scientists, correlations of temperature and greenhouse gas concentrations indicate that the greenhouse effect has had little, if any, effect on global climate change. Scientists representing the Marshall Institute believe that the greenhouse warming produced from a doubling of CO_2 in the next century will be "less than 1.5 degree C (2.7 degree F), and may be as small as 0.5 degrees C (0.9 degree F)." They believe that differing levels of solar activity provide a much more likely explanation for increases in average global temperature.[3]

2. National Academy of Sciences, *Policy Implications of Greenhouse Warming*. (Washington D.C.: National Academy Press, 1991), pgs. 18, 93.
3. George C. Marshall Institute, *Global Warming Update: Recent Scientific Findings* (Washington, D.C.: the George C. Marshall Institute, 1992), pgs. 25-26.

Consequences of Greenhouse Warming

The National Academy of Sciences report categorized climate change predictions into three categories reflecting different levels of plausibility:

Highly plausible:	Global average surface warming
	Global average precipitation increase
	Reduction in sea ice
	Surface winter warming at high altitudes
Plausible:	Global sea level rise
	Intensification of summer mid-altitude drying
	High-latitude precipitation increase
Highly uncertain:	Local details of climate change
	Regional distribution of precipitation
	Regional vegetation changes
	Increase in tropical storm intensity or frequency

The report concludes that any of the changes above would vary significantly from region to region and would be difficult to predict. "The nature and magnitude of the weather conditions and events that might accompany greenhouse warming at any particular location in the future are extremely uncertain."[4]

Adapting To Climate Change

Even if some of the climate changes listed above occur, it is not clear how human and natural systems will adapt to them. Adaptation would depend on two basic factors: the *extent* and the *rate* of climate change, and would vary from region to region. Some regions might benefit from the hypothesized effects of global warming, while some might be harmed. It is generally acknowledged that it would not be difficult for industry and agriculture in industrial countries to adapt to gradual climate change. However, poorer countries would have more difficulty since they have less economic sophistication and flexibility, information, and expertise.

While most scientists currently believe that there could be some adverse regional effects from greenhouse warming, some scientists contend that the effects of greenhouse warming would actually be *positive*. This view, based on natural experiments as opposed to theoretical climate models, believes that a more carbon-rich environment coupled with overall increased precipitation levels would greatly enhance tree and plant growth. This would result in more organic matter being returned to the soil, which would set off a host of beneficial consequences.[5]

---

4. National Academy of Sciences, p. 76.
5. David D. Kemp, *Global Environmental Issues* (London and New York: Routledge, 1990, pgs. 160-161.)

Policy Implications of Greenhouse Warming

Because of the uncertainty surrounding greenhouse warming, policy implications are varied and complex. However, it is possible to identify three broad categories of public policy responses to greenhouse warming.

1. *Do Nothing* – Continue to finance some additional research, but do not incur any major costs until more is known about the extent and implications of greenhouse warming. For example, in the early 1980s, a rise of more than several meters in the sea level due to global warming was considered a possibility. The estimated range by 1990 was much less, from 0.2 meters to 0.7 meters. Some scientific articles even predict that global warming will actually cause sea level to *fall,* as warmer air at the poles allows frigid air there to hold more moisture, resulting in more snowfall.[6] Also, ice has more physical volume than water, though ice melted off land and mountains will definitely increase sea levels. Costly CO_2 mitigation policies, based on some of the dire prediction in the early 1980s, would have been unwise given more recent research results.

2. *Take Limited Action To Reduce Greenhouse Emissions* – Adopt precautionary measures that make modest immediate reduction in greenhouse emissions and make modest investments now that will reduce the costs of larger future reduction, should they become necessary. Such policies include elimination of subsidies for energy use and deforestation, significant funding of additional research, and broader dissemination of information about energy-saving technologies.

3. *Take Immediate and Significant Action to Stabilize or Reduce Greenhouse Emissions.* This view believes that the problem is serious enough to warrant immediate and significant action to reduce greenhouse emissions. This statement by environmentalist Jan Beyea of the National Audubon Society illustrates the view called the Precautionary Principle: "Although we cannot be sure that these projections (about increasing greenhouse warming) are correct, we must act as if they are correct. We cannot take the risk that the global climate models (GCMs) are wrong."[7] Proponents want governments to enforce stringent policies for reducing greenhouse gases, including specific emission reduction targets and definite time tables.

Economic Solutions. Policy analysts emphasize the importance of using economic incentives to address (prevent or reverse) global warming. Full cost pricing is essential. This means that consumers pay the full costs, including environmental damages (waste disposal, pollution abatement), of the goods and services they purchase. To encourage full cost pricing, economists recommend either of two market-based approaches: 1. cap-and-trade programs similar to the Clean Air Act Amendment's SO_2 allowances trading system, where overly clean companies can

---

6. George C. Marshall Institute, *Global Warming* Update, pgs. 22-24.
7. Jan Beyea, "Energy Policy and Global Warning," in Richard Wyman (ed.), *Global Climate Change and Life on Earth* (New York: Chapman and Hall, 1991), p. 224.

sell emissions credits to under-performing businesses, all within an overall cap on their industry's collective total; or 2. pollution taxes per unit of emissions. Distinguished economist William Nordhaus of Yale University estimates that a carbon tax of $8 per ton would stabilize long-term CO_2 concentrations at 550 ppm (double the preindustrial level) and a $26 per ton carbon tax would limit concentrations to 450 ppm.

In a thorough analysis of world environmental issues, the *World Development Report* (www.worldbank.org/wdr/2000/fullreport.html) stresses that the choice among policy options to address greenhouse warming must depend on the relative *marginal costs* and *marginal benefits* of the options. Policies must not severely hamper legitimate economic development since development provides the financial capital necessary for meeting environmental challenges. "Autonomous, self-interested state actions can improve both the environment and economic performance, as emphasized in the *World Development Report 1992*."[8] For this reason, the *World Development Report 1992* recommended only limited greenhouse reduction policies.

The balance of the evidence does not support a case for doing nothing, but neither does it support stringent measures to reduce emissions now – the costs are too high in relation to the prospective benefits…Such an insurance policy, which would go further than economic efficiency alone would dictate, is justified by uncertainty about the physical and economic effects of climate change and by the lags between action and response.[9]

Summary

The critical conclusion that emerges from a current study of this controversial issue is the large measure of *uncertainty* that currently surrounds it. Although human-caused global warming is accepted in the popular media as a scientific fact, in fact, it is not. At this time there are simply too many uncertainties. For example, Sallie Baliunas of the Harvard-Smithsonian Center for Astrophysics, points out three important uncertainties surrounding the predictions of computer models.

> At first glance, it seems that the observed warming occurred due to the increases in the minor greenhouse gases in the last 100 years and is good evidence for the validity of projections of global warming from human activities.
>
> That conclusion is insupportable for several reasons. First, at least half of the warming seen in the surface temperature record occurred before about 1940, while most of the greenhouse gas increase in the atmosphere occurred after 1940. That means that *most of the temperature rise of the last 100 years occurred before the substantial increases in greenhouse gases in the atmosphere from human activities.* Of the 0.5 C rise observed, at most only one or two tenths of a degree can be attributed to increased greenhouse gases.
>
> A second problem is the uncertainty of the urban-heat-island effect in the temperature records: temperature measurements made in growing, modern cities can read excess warmth due to the effects of machinery, pavement, tree-cutting, etc. A correction, as best as possible, can been made, but the process can introduce a systematic error in the

---

8. World Bank, *World Development Report,* (New York: Oxford University Press, 1999/2000). p.90.
9. World Bank, *World Development Report* (New York: Oxford University Press, 1992), p. 161.

average record.

Another uncertainty comes from uneven coverage in the surface records. Good records with near-continual coverage for the last 100 years apply to only 18 per cent of the surface. Better coverage exists today of the surface; still, the Polar Regions as well as vast areas of the southern and tropical oceans are not adequately sampled.[10]

The uncertainty — and complexity — surrounding the global warming issue makes it very difficult for policymakers, who must decide whether or not to implement costly greenhouse gas reduction policies which will yield indeterminate results far into the future. As the *World Development Report* says, "The benefits of efforts to prevent climate change will become apparent only in the long term, while the costs of such mitigation must be paid today."[11] Until there is definite scientific evidence about the effects of greenhouse gases on the environment, public policies dealing with global warming will remain contentious.

---

10. Sallie Baliunas, "Hot Times or Hot Air: The Sun in the Science of Global Warming," Marshall Institute, August 7, 1998. (See http://www.marshall.org/article.php?id=11.)
11. World Bank, *World Development Report*, (New York: Oxford University Press, 1999/2000). p. 97.

Global Warming Vocabulary

Adaptation The adjustment by both human and natural systems to new climatic conditions

Carbon Dioxide CO_2, the most abundant greenhouse gas

Carbon Cycle A process occurring in nature that maintains a balance between the release of carbon compounds from their sources and their absorption in sinks, such as oceans and forests

Carbon Sink Natural systems in the environment, such as forests and oceans, that absorb carbon compounds such as CO_2. Oceans are the largest active carbon sink.

CFCs Chlorofluorocarbons, the only manmade greenhouse gas; released from refrigeration units, aerosol sprays, and insulating foams; present in the atmosphere in small, but increasing concentrations

Cost Benefit Analysis A technique used in economic analysis to compare the costs and benefits of various policy options

Energy Efficiency The amount of energy it takes to do a certain amount of work

Fossil Fuels Nonrenewable fuels, such as coal, oil, and natural gas. All contain carbon.

GCMs General circulation models; complex mathematical computer models used to predict global climate change

Global Warming The possible increase in average global temperature resulting from greater concentrations of greenhouse gases

Greenhouse Effect The warming influence produced by greenhouse gases as they absorb energy radiated from the earth. Without this effect, the earth's temperatures would be much cooler.

Greenhouse Gases Trace gases, such as carbon dioxide, methane, nitrous oxide, and CFCs

Photosynthesis   A process shared by all green plants by which solar energy is converted to chemical energy. Carbon dioxide taken in by the leaves is broken down into carbon, which is retained by the plant, and oxygen, which is released into the atmosphere. In this capacity, plants serve as a carbon sink.

Spillover Cost
(Negative Externality)   When the harmful effects of pollution are imposed on individuals not directly involved in the buying and selling decisions that caused the pollution

Trade-off   Giving up some of one thing in order to get some of another. For example, countries that implement significant greenhouse emission reduction policies are trading off economic growth for protection against possible climate change. Countries that do not reduce emissions are trading off protection against possible climate change for more economic growth.

Teaching Instructions

Overview

The specific teaching activities in this unit do not necessarily have to be done in order. However, the Case Study should probably be done toward the end of the unit when students have mastered much of the basic information.

Some of the basic information to teach your students is in the Facts About Global Warming section. Other information is available from a variety of sources. Encourage your students to research this information on their own. The Further Investigations section suggests a variety of research activities.

Some of the key economic concepts your students should learn are described below in the Important Concepts To Emphasize section. The Key Questions To Ask Students section should also be helpful.

Important Concepts To Emphasize

1. **Carbon Dioxide Emissions as a Spillover Cost.** A carbon tax is a current public policy consideration because many believe that carbon dioxide emissions from fossil fuels contribute to the problem of global warming, with potentially great societal costs. To the extent that this is true, CO_2 emissions are a spillover cost (external cost) of production since the costs of producing goods and services using fossil fuels do not reflect accurately the full social costs of production. The tax is an attempt to *internalize* the negative external affects of carbon dioxide emissions.

2. **Is a Carbon Tax a Good Idea?** *If* it is determined that global warming is indeed a danger, a carbon tax may be a good policy option for several reasons. First, because the tax would cover CO_2 *emissions*, firms would have an economic incentive to reduce their emissions. Second, a carbon tax can achieve overall CO_2 reductions at far less overall cost to society than "command and control" regulations. Not only are administrative costs lower, but a properly designed tax would encourage emission reductions by those firms that could accomplish the reductions at a low cost. Third, it is a "corrective tax," one that improves the functioning of the market by internalizing the presumed harmful spillover costs of CO_2 emissions. Fourth, a higher price for fossil fuels (to reflect their full social costs to the environment) would reduce their amount demanded and would encourage the development of alternative energy sources.

   There would also be some disadvantages to a carbon tax. The tax would probably result in a greater burden on lower income groups. It would also have a very adverse effect on states that rely heavily on fossil fuel production, such as West Virginia. Also, a carbon tax would increase product prices in the United States and would have a negative impact on the United States balance of trade. This is because the United States uses more energy per unit of GDP than Japan and most European countries. This high energy/GDP ratio occurs for several reasons. First, the United States is a very large country that depends heavily on long distance freight and passenger travel. Also, the United States has extreme climate variability, resulting in high energy use for heating and cooling.

This heating and cooling impact is significant because land in the United States is not as scarce as in these other countries, and houses tend to be much larger.

3. **Opportunity Cost and Trade-Offs:** Any policy choice will involve opportunity costs and trade-offs among policy goals. Tax monies are limited and choices must be made among competing alternatives. Monies used for climate research cannot be used for cancer research. Also, different policies will always reflect different social goals. For example, advocating a "do nothing at this time" policy towards global warming will probably favor economic growth over certain environmental goals.

4. **Marginal Benefit/Marginal Cost:** The real issue in the case study is not the advantages or disadvantages of the carbon tax, but the more fundamental issue of whether the United States should act to mitigate greenhouse emissions in the midst of major uncertainty about climate change. If scientists determined that there were some adverse effects from increasing greenhouse gases, would avoiding these effects be worth the enormous cost of not using cheap and abundant fossil fuel resources? The availability of these fuels has enabled many people throughout the world to raise their standard of living and can enable many more to do so. Is the marginal benefit that we would obtain from mitigating some global warming worth the significant marginal cost of what it would take to do so? That is the real economic question.

Teaching Suggestions

Review information about global warming with your students. Discuss the information provided in the Facts About Global Warming section. Also, discuss the data presented in Table 1: Carbon Dioxide Emissions. (page 141). The data reveal interesting differences and implications.

ACTIVITY 1: GREENHOUSE WARMING: WHAT IS IT? Encourage students to do neat, careful work. Encourage them to research various sources to get information.

ACTIVITY 2: HOW MUCH IS ENOUGH? Follow the directions given to you very carefully. It should take no more than 20-30 minutes, depending on the amount of discussion/debriefing.

ACTIVITY 3: ANALYZING GREENHOUSE DATA. The key point to emphasize in this activity is that some scientists believe experimental temperature data do not support the fact of global warming as predicted by computer models. The data reveal that most of the warming during the past century occurred *before* 1940. However, it was *after* 1940 that the greatest increases in greenhouse gases occurred. This teaching activity reveals why there is so much scientific uncertainty surrounding the greenhouse effect. See answers to Activity 3.

ACTIVITY 4: FURTHER INVESTIGATIONS. Encourage students to do research on their own. There have been many articles in the popular media on this controversial topic. Encourage students to share information they have learned with their classmates.

ACTIVITY 5: DEBATING THE ISSUES. Students can debate orally or can present their views in a written assignment.

ACTIVITY 6: EEE ACTIONS: YOU CAN MAKE A DIFFERENCE! Encourage students to implement some of the suggested activities.

ACTIVITY 7: CASE STUDY: THE CASE OF THE CARBON TAX. You can do the case study as a large or small group activity. Students should use the Decision Worksheet and Decision Grid from Unit 1. Discuss different group decisions.

Key Questions to Ask Students

1. Why are greenhouse gases considered by some to be a spillover (external) cost? (*Some believe high concentrations of these gases will lead to harmful effects on society, such as climate disruption and flooding. Producers do not have to bear the costs of these adverse effects in production; they are imposed on others.*)

2. Assuming that the greenhouse effect is a real problem, what are the advantages and disadvantages of a carbon tax? (*Advantages: taxing emissions creates incentives to reduce emissions; higher fuel prices as a result of the tax reduce the quantity of fossil fuel purchased and stimulate research in new, less carbon-intensive fuel technologies; it corrects inefficiencies in the market by dealing with negative externalities; it is less costly to administer than "command and control" regulations. Disadvantages: would raise the prices of domestically produced goods and services; would make us less competitive in international markets; would have a disproportionate impact on individuals with low incomes; would especially harm the economies of certain regions of the United States which produce fossil fuels.*)

3. What are some of the goods and services that will become more expensive if a carbon tax is imposed? (*Electricity, gasoline, all goods and services that require energy for production.*) If your income stayed constant, what might you have to give up? Is a reduction in carbon worth it to you? Why or why not? (*Answers will vary.*)

4. What are some major social and economic goals that are involved in the issue of greenhouse warming? (*Environmental quality, economic growth, jobs and employment, regional equity, price stability, trade competitiveness.*)

5. What are some of the trade-offs among goals that arise in analyzing this issue. (*Example: stressing environmental quality through policies to reduce greenhouse gases means accepting less progress toward the goals of economic growth, income, and trade competitiveness, and vice versa.*)

6. What is the opportunity cost of "doing nothing" to alleviate increases in greenhouse gases? (*Giving up the benefits of having fewer greenhouse gases in the atmosphere.*) What is the opportunity cost of implementing rigorous policies to reduce greenhouse emissions? (*Giving up whatever else could be done with the resources it would take to implement these policies.*)

Table 1: Carbon Dioxide Emissions from Fossil Fuels
(1988 and 2003 Estimates – Metric Tons)

Country	Total CO_2 Emissions (million tons/yr.)		Per Capita CO_2 Emissions		CO_2 Emissions per unit of GDP (million tons CO_2/$1000 GDP)	
	1988	2003	1988	2003	1988	2003
Canada	475.1	600.2	17.7	19.1	.90	.80
China	2236.3	3541.0	2.1	2.7	6.01	2.58
Hungry	72.0	58.4	6.89	5.9	1.62	1.13
France	320.1	409.2	5.9	6.8	.34	.30
Japan	989.3	1205.6	8.1	9.4	.35	.25
Saudi Arabia	199.9	327.4	14.2	13.5	1.45	1.60
United Kingdom	559.2	564.6	9.9	9.5	.80	.37
United States	4804.1	5802.1	19.4	20.0	.98	.56
Russia	N/A	1606.4	N/A	11.2	N/A	5.24
Italy	396.0	465.5	7.0	8.11	.45	.42

Source: Energy Information Agency. http://www.eia.doe.gov/iea/carbon.html

Unit 4

Global Warming

Student Activities

Activity 1

Greenhouse Warming: What Is It?

Situation:

An alien from another planet has just arrived and is perplexed by the controversy surrounding the greenhouse effect and global warming. Here's how you can help:

Task 1: Draw a diagram illustrating the greenhouse effect. Label it carefully.

Task 2: Below your diagram write a concise paragraph that explains the diagram. Write neatly, using correct English! Use the back of this worksheet if necessary.

Activity 2

How Much Is Enough?

Overview

A similar version of this motivating group activity appears in Unit 1 on water pollution. ("The White Glove Test," p. 40) In both versions, students use marginal analysis to address the difficult questions, "How clean is a clean environment?" and "How much are we willing to pay for a clean environment?" While carbon dioxide and other greenhouse gases are not "pollutants," students can use the same marginal analysis to help determine how many scarce productive resources a society should devote to reducing greenhouse gas emissions.

Learning Objectives

After completing this activity, students will understand that:

1.   It requires costly productive resources to reduce greenhouse emissions.

2.   Individuals and societies will reduce greenhouse gas emissions by first doing the *least* costly greenhouse reduction activities.

3.   It is too expensive in terms of opportunity cost to eliminate greenhouse gas emissions completely.

4.   Scientists and individuals differ on what is a "safe" level of greenhouse gas emissions.

Notes to the Teacher

It is important to distribute enough "greenhouse emissions." You'll be surprised at how well 25 students clean up a classroom in one minute! You may even want to shorten the cleanup time.

Option: You may want to distribute fewer "greenhouse emissions" and let a group of 4-5 students do the cleaning. This works very well.

Directions

1.   When your students are gone, litter the classroom floor with a variety of different materials representing "greenhouse gases." Possible suggestions: balls of scrap paper, popcorn, wood shavings, small dots of paper from a paper punch, paper chips, rice, dry grits, glitter. *It is important to include a significant amount of tiny, "difficult to pick up" types of materials, such as dry grits or glitter.*

2.   When students arrive, tell them that the items on the floor represent the "excess" greenhouse gases in the environments. Tell the students that, to reduce the likelihood of global warming, you would appreciate their help in reducing these emissions.

3. Allow three approximate one-minute rounds to "reduce excess emissions." After each round, record on the board the types of items that were found. Discuss what greenhouse gases these items represent. By the end of the third round, most "emissions" should be gone.

4. After the third round ask, "Have we eliminated the greenhouse emissions?" After students agree, examine the floor carefully and discover some small bits of glitter, etc. Tell students that some greenhouse emissions still remain. They haven't removed all of them! Ask students if they want to continue reducing emissions.

5. Discussion questions:

    a. What kinds of greenhouse "gases" did you find? What real greenhouse gases do these represent? *(Identify various items: carbon dioxide, methane, nitrous oxide, CFCs, water vapor).*

    b. What did you have to do to reduce the greenhouse emissions*? (We had to work. It took time. To do a thorough job we needed **capital**, such as a broom or vacuum cleaner. In real life, it would take **costly productive resources** to reduce these emissions.)*

    c. What type of emissions did you reduce first? Why? *(The large items. It cost less in terms of time and effort to reduce them first. The benefit was also greatest.)*

    d. Why did you say that the excess emissions were eliminated when they actually weren't? *(It seemed like most were eliminated. Only tiny items, such as dry grits or glitter, remained.)*

    e. Why don't we spend more time reducing these remaining "greenhouse emissions?" (It takes too much time. The **opportunity cost** is too great. We have other important things we need to do.)

    f. In real public policy decisions, to avoid possible global warming why don't we take drastic steps to reduce greenhouse emissions? *(The **marginal cost** of doing so would probably exceed the **marginal benefit**. At some point, greenhouse emissions would be reduced enough. After that point, scarce productive resources would best be used elsewhere, such as for education, roads, cancer research, etc.)*

(An original version of this activity appeared in the article, "A Clean Environment, A Matter of Choice," by Robert W. Reinke and Diance W. Reinke, in the *Elementary Economist,* Spring 1989.)

Activity 3

Analyzing Greenhouse Data

Directions: In this activity, you will analyze and graph data on observed global temperatures and CO_2 concentrations. Then you will answer questions about these data.

Task 1: On the graph below, plot the data in Table 2. Label the horizontal axis "Year" and label the vertical axis "CO_2 Concentration." (See http://www.grida.no/climate/vital/07.htm.)

Table 2: Atmosphere Concentration of CO_2 During the Last 250 Years

Year	CO_2 Concentration (parts per million-ppm)
1750	282 ppm
1800	283 ppm
1850	290 ppm
1900	297 ppm
1950	312 ppm
1980	335 ppm
1990	350 ppm
2000	370 ppm

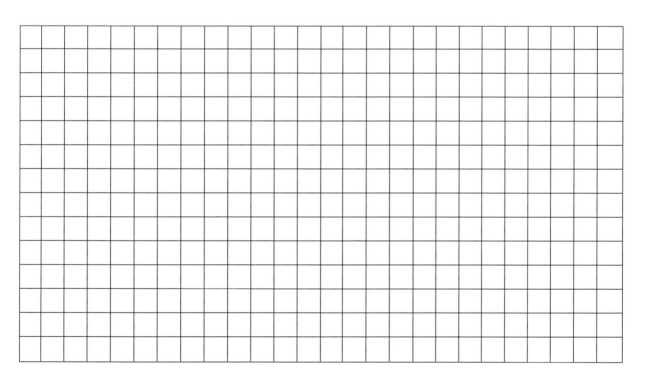

a.   What pattern or trend do you notice in CO_2 concentration? During what years is the trend most evident? _____

_____

Task 2: Table 3 gives actual average global temperature changes during the past 110 years, using 1890 as a base year. Below Table 3 is a graph showing CO_2 concentration during this same time period. Plot the data in Table 3 on the graph below. Then answer the questions.

Table 3: Observed (Actual) Global Average Temperature Change
(Pre 2000 data found in "Climate Impact of Increasing Atmospheric Carbon Dioxide," *Science*, August 28, 1991.)

Year	Global Average Temperature (Observed Change from 1890 – Degrees C)
1890	0.00
1900	0.18
1910	0.20
1920	0.22
1930	0.43
1940	0.54
1950	0.48
1960	0.43
1970	0.40
1980	0.55
1990	0.56
2000	0.56

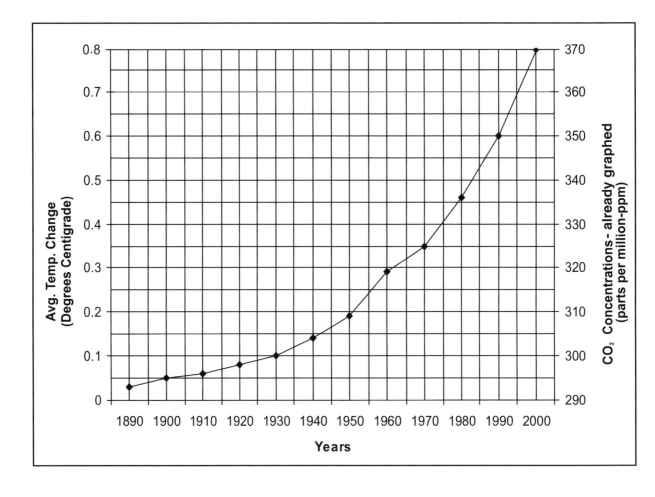

a. During what time period was the observed temperature <u>increase</u> the greatest? _____.
    _____ What period of time shows a <u>decrease</u> in observed temperature?
    _____

b. What time period shows the greatest increase in CO_2 concentrations? _____
    _____
    _____

c. Examine the data carefully. Do the data support the conclusion that increasing
    greenhouse emissions are responsible for the 0.56 degree Centigrade increase in
    observed temperature during the past 110 years? Explain your reasoning below. Discuss
    your conclusions with your teacher and your classmates.

    _____
    _____
    _____
    _____
    _____
    _____
    _____

d. What are some other natural phenomena that possibly could explain increases in
    temperature? _____
    _____
    _____
    _____

e. Assume you are a weather scientist and are called before a Congressional committee to
    testify on the global warming issue. Would you recommend public policies that would
    require reductions in greenhouse gas emissions? Explain your position and support it
    with scientific evidence.

    _____
    _____
    _____
    _____
    _____
    _____
    _____

f. Did the *cost* of greenhouse reduction policies affect your decision in e. above? Explain.
    _____
    _____

149

Activity 4

Further Investigations

1.   Write or call your United States Representative or Senator and request information about global warming. Indicate you are particularly interested in legislation that addresses this issue.

2.   Write various environmental organizations requesting information about greenhouse warming. Analyze their views. What remedies do they recommend for global warming? Do the same for industry groups like coal and petroleum companies. Compare and contrast the difference in viewpoints.

3.   Cut out articles from news magazines or newspapers that address global warming. Put them on the bulletin board. Note any new research findings and indicate differences from previous findings.

4.   Interview other teachers in your school. Ask them these and other similar questions:

   a.   Can you explain greenhouse warming?
   b.   Do you think greenhouse warming is a real problem?
   c.   Do you think the United States should adopt policies to reduce greenhouse emissions?
   d.   What policies do you recommend? Give specific examples.
   e.   Should the United States impose a carbon tax on fossil fuels to help reduce greenhouse gases?
   f.   Have you made any changes in your personal lifestyle to help reduce greenhouse emissions? Why or why not?
   g.   Should the United States pay other countries to help them reduce their emissions? Why or why not?

   Analyze and discuss the teachers' responses. Do they generally agree in their responses? Where is the disagreement the greatest?

5.   Some scientists believe that more carbon dioxide in the atmosphere will increase plant growth and return more organic matter to the soil, resulting in many beneficial effects. The leading spokesman for this group of scientists is Sherwood Idso. (see www.Co2science.org). Research more about this point of view and report these findings to the class.

Activity 5

Debating The Issues

Below are some controversial statements to debate with your classmates.

1. The United States should take immediate and forceful steps to reduce CO_2 emissions even if this means putting some coal miners out of work.

2. The United States should agree to definite emission reductions and submit to definite timetables.

3. Since the richer, industrial countries of the world are responsible for most CO_2 emissions and have benefited from them, these countries should now pay poorer countries to help them reduce CO_2 emissions.

4. The United States should wait until more definite research has accumulated before trying to reduce CO_2 emissions.

5. To reduce our dependence on oil (and thus reduce greenhouse emissions), the United States government should require automobile companies to produce automobiles that get 100 miles per gallon.

6. An environment rich in CO_2 would not be harmful to the earth, but actually would be very beneficial. We should be doing nothing at all to discourage CO_2 emissions. If anything, we should *encourage* them!

7. Burning gasoline emits carbon dioxide. To encourage people to use less gasoline, there should be a $.75 per gallon tax increase on gasoline, even if this tax hurts low income people more than others.

8. The U.S. should sign the Kyoto Protocol Agreement to reduce greenhouse gases.

Activity 6

EEE Actions -
You Can Make A Difference!

We all engage in activities in our daily lives that directly or indirectly increase the amount of carbon dioxide in the atmosphere. As you have learned in this unit, some people feel this contributes to global warming. If you want to increase your energy efficiency by reducing the amount of fossil fuels you use, you can do the following:

1. When feasible, walk or ride a bicycle instead of using a motor vehicle.

2. Do all you can to save energy in your home by:

    • Conducting a home energy audit to determine energy loss.
    • Encouraging your parents to buy energy efficient appliances.
    • Using fluorescent light bulbs – they cost more initially, but should save money in the long run.
    • Turning off lights as you leave rooms.
    • Using air conditioning only if you feel it is really necessary.
    • Not overheating the water in the hot water heater – a temperature of 130 degrees is usually sufficient.
    • Installing insulation in your attic.

3. Use public transportation whenever possible.

4. Encourage members in your family to buy automobiles that get good gas mileage. Also, make sure that automobiles in your family are properly tuned and that tires are inflated properly.

5. Trees use carbon dioxide and produce oxygen. If possible, plant a tree where you live.

6. Recycling certain kinds of materials (especially aluminum) can save a lot of energy.

7. Reusing products can also save energy. Try to avoid disposable products.

Activity 7

Case Study
The Case of the Carbon Tax

Student Directions:

1. In the case study below, legislators are dealing with an issue that is receiving much attention – greenhouse warming. The issue is whether to impose a "carbon tax" on fossil fuels such as coal, oil, and natural gas.

2. Analyze the case study below and use the Decision Worksheet and the Decision Grid to help determine whether such a tax would be a good idea. Be prepared to defend your decision!

SCENARIO

Congressman Samuel Peabody of New York was convinced that global warming was the most important issue facing the United States and the world. He was very concerned that rising levels of greenhouse gases, especially carbon dioxide (CO_2), would cause increasing average global temperatures. The result would be more droughts, famines, flooded coastlines, and increased tropic storm intensity. "If we don't do something now to stop increasing CO_2 emissions, it could be the end of the world as we know it," he emphasized in a debate on the House floor.

His solution was to introduce House Bill (H.B.) 107, a law that would impose a "carbon tax" on three fossil fuels: coal, oil, and natural gas. The tax would reflect the fuel's carbon content since carbon content was roughly proportional to the amount of CO_2 released when fossil fuels are burned. The tax would be imposed at the port of entry for imported fuels and at the point of primary production for fuels produced in the United States. The bill would set the carbon charge at $100 per ton, phased in over a period of 10 years. Some of the enormous tax revenues would be used for environmental research and cleaning up the environment even more. To lessen the overall financial burden of the carbon tax, H.B. 107 calls for some reductions in social security and income taxes.

Congressman Peabody insisted that according to Congressional Budget Office (CBO) estimates, this would reduce CO_2 emissions by approximately 20 percent by the year 2012. The much higher prices for fuels resulting from the tax would force people to be more energy efficient and it would encourage the development of renewable energy sources, such as wind and solar energy. "This bill will ensure that our children and grandchildren have a safe environment to live in. It's the least we can do for future generations."

Congresswoman Phyllis Adams of West Virginia strongly disagreed. "I also think we should care for our environment," she said, "but we're not even sure that greenhouse warming is a fact. It's just a theory based on computer models. Do we want to spend billions to stop something that may never happen? According to the CBO, your carbon tax would hurt economic growth and employment. The overall effect of the tax, despite some social security and income tax reductions, would be to reduce people's real incomes. That is especially hard on poor people. Also, certain regions of the country would be devastated, like the coal mining economies of West Virginia and southern Indiana. Let's face it – it's just too expensive forcing our whole economy away from fossil fuels. Until we know more about greenhouse warming, our best policy option is to do nothing at this time. I'm strongly opposed to H.B. 107."

Congressman Gerald Williams of California also had concerns about the economic costs of H.B. 107. He introduced H.B. 219, the "Greenhouse Warming Insurance Policy" bill. It called for a $10 per ton carbon tax. The tax revenues would fund significant increases in research in the area of both greenhouse climate change and energy efficiency. The bill also included additional funding to distribute this information to producers and citizens. According to Congressman Williams, "This bill costs much less than H.B. 107, and gives us more time to study the issue. It also helps us become more energy efficient in case greenhouse warming becomes a more severe problem."

Rep. Adams still disagreed, "It's still throwing too much money at a problem that may not even exist. There are other more important needs for our tax monies, such as education, better highways, and medical research."

Rep. Peabody was also upset by H.B. 219. "We cannot afford to wait for the results of global warming research. If we want to stop future greenhouse warming, we must act *now* in a *significant* way. This won't help much at all."

The vote is next week. It promises to be close. Which policy do you prefer? How would you vote?

Answers to Selected Teaching Activities:

Activity 1: Greenhouse Warming: What Is It?

Refer to the diagram and explanation in the Facts About Global Warming section at the beginning of this unit.

Activity 2: How Much Is Enough?

The key idea to emphasize in this activity is that it is not possible to eliminate greenhouse emissions (or pollution!) completely. The key question to ask is "What is an acceptable level of greenhouse gas emissions?" What makes policy making so difficult is the great *uncertainty* about the effect of greenhouse gases on global climate change. At some point, it will become counterproductive to keep reducing greenhouse emissions. This is because reducing additional emissions becomes increasingly more costly while the additional benefits from reducing emissions begin to decrease. For a more complete explanation, review the concept of marginalism on page 13.

Activity 3: Analyzing Greenhouse Data

Task 1: a. The obvious trend is the increase in CO_2 concentrations. The greatest increase has taken place during the past 50 years. b. The primary reason is the burning of fossil fuels that has resulted from increased industrial activity.

Task 2: a. The greatest temperature increase was prior to 1940. b. The greatest decrease in temperature was from 1940 to 1970. c. The data show that, in a *rough* sense, the temperature increase during the past century has occurred as CO_2 levels have increased. However, the actual increase in temperature occurred *before* the greatest increase in CO_2 concentrations.

For example, Sallie of Baliunas of the Harvard-Smithsonian Center for Astrophysics concludes: "As a result of looking at the temperature information, one concludes two things: 1. the climate scenarios exaggerate the warming that should have already occurred (and likely also the future warming) as a result of increased greenhouse gasses; and 2. most of the warming this century cannot be caused by increased greenhouse gases because the warming predates the greatest increases in the greenhouse gases."[16] (See Summary, page 134.)

d. The data record indicates that some other factors are probably involved, such as 1. the cooling effects of increased atmospheric pollution, 2. the delayed warming of the oceans, 3. the cooling effect of an increasing cloud cover caused by the greenhouse effect, and 4. increased solar activity. Students may want to research these and other explanations.

---

16. Sallie Balinas, "The Sun in the Science of Global Warming," www.marshall.org/article.php?id=11

The most mentioned phenomenon is the effect of solar activity. According to the Marshall Institute, "The very close correlation between the solar changes and the changes in temperature suggests that the sun has been the controlling influence on climate in the last 100 years, with the greenhouse effect playing a smaller role."[17]

e. Students who favor emission reduction policies will rely more on the predictions of the GCMs and the belief that the risk of *not* reducing emissions is too great. Students who favor few or no reduction policies will rely more on experimental data, which show no definitive correlation between greenhouse emissions and global warming.

f. Cost would definitely be a factor. Costly greenhouse reduction policies may not be worth the additional benefits they produce.

Activity 7: Case Study: The Case of the Carbon Tax

Below is a suggested Solution Grid. As in the other case studies, you and your students may disagree about different cell marking. Make sure that you discuss the questions in the Key Questions To Ask Students section. Some of the questions relate directly to the Case Study.

Decision-Making Grid Answer Key **The Case of the Carbon Tax**					
	Criteria				
Alternatives	**Reduces CO$_2$**	**Cost**	**Fairness**	**Economic Growth**	**Promote Energy Efficiency**
Implement HB107 ($100/ton carbon tax)	+ +	− −	−	−	+ +
Do nothing at this time	− −	+ +	+	+	−
Implement HB219 (Insurance Policy Bill)	+	−	?	?	+

---

17. George C. Marshall Institute, *Global Warming Update: Recent Scientific Findings* (Washington, DC: The George C. Marshall Institute, 1992), pgs. 25-26.

EEE Resources

General Resources

United States Environmental Protection Agency - www.epa.gov

Indiana Department of Education – www.doe.state.in.us

Indiana Council for Economic Education - www.econed-in.org

Indiana Department of Environmental Management – www.in.gov/idem

Indiana Department of Natural Resources - www.state.in.us/dnr

National Council on Economic Education - www.ncee.net

National Geographic Society - www.nationalgeographic.com

Water Quality Resources

Union of Concerned Scientists   www.ucsusa.org

American Groundwater Trust - www.agwt.org

American Water Works Association - www.awwa.org

Federal Drinking Water Hotline – www.epa.gov/safewater/hotline/index.html

Izaak Walton League of America – www.iwla.org

Lake Michigan Federation – www.great-lakes.net/lakes/michigan

Alliance for the Great Lakes - www.lakemichigan.org

United States Geological Survey – www.usgs.gov

Water Environment Federation – www.wef.org

World Bank (*World Development Report* available) – www.worldbank.org

U.S. National Oceanic and Atmospheric Administration - www.noaa.gov

Forest Resources

American Forest Foundation – www.affoundation.org

American Forest and Paper Association – www.afandpa.org

American Tree Farm System – www.treefarmsystem.org

Indiana Wildlife Federation – www.indianawildlife.org

Indiana Department of Natural Resources, Division of Forestry – www.in.gov/dnr/forestry

National Arbor Day Foundation – www.arborday.org

National Audubon Society – www.audubon.org

National Wildlife Federation – www.nwf.org

Society of American Foresters – www.safnet.org

The Wilderness Society – www.wilderness.org

United States Department of Agriculture – Forest Services – www.fs.fed.us

United States Fish and Wildlife Service, Department of the Interior – www.fws.gov/index.html

Energy Resources

The Alliance to Save Energy – www.ase.org

American Council for an Energy Efficient Economy – www.aceee.org

American Electric Power (AEP) – www.aep.com

American Electric Power (AEP) Teacher Grants –
www.aep.com/about/community/teacherGrants/default.htm

American Solar Energy Society – www.ases.org

American Wind Energy Association – www.awea.org

Duke Energy (formerly CINERGY/PSI Energy) – www.duke-energy.com

Citizens Gas – www.citizensgas.com

Energy Efficiency and Renewable Energy – www.eere.energy.gov

Electricity Information Card - www.eia.doe.gov/neic/brochure/elecinfocard.html

Electric Universe (for kids) – www.electricuniverse.com

Energy Information Administration: U.S. Government – www.eia.doe.gov

Energy Kid's Page - www.eia.doe.gov/kids/energyfacts/index.html

Geothermal Education Office – www.geothermal.marin.org

Indiana Michigan Power – www.indianamichiganpower.com

Indianapolis Power and Light Company – www.ipalco.com

National Energy Foundation – www.nef1.org

National Hydropower Association – www.hydro.org

Northern Indiana Public Service Company – www.nipsco.nisource.com

NEED (National Energy Education Development Project) – www.need.org

Renewable Fuels Association – www.ethanolrfa.org

Solar Energy Industries Association – www.seia.org

Vectren – www.vectren.com

Air Quality Resources

Conservation Law Foundation – www.clf.org

Air & Waste Management Association – www.awma.org

Center for Environmental Information – www.ceinfo.org

Competitive Enterprise Institute – www.cei.org

EPA Global Warming Site – http://yosemite.epa.gov/oar/globalwarming.nsf

Global Warming International Center – www.globalwarming.net

Global Warming Kids Site (United States Environmental Protection Agency) – www.epa.gov/globalwarming/kids

Indiana Department of Environmental Management – www.state.in.us/idem

Marshall Institute – www.marshall.org

National Academy of Sciences - www.nasonline.org

Natural Resources Defense Council - www.nrdc.org

The John Heinz III Center for Science, Economics, and the Environment – www.heinzctr.org

The Cooler Heads Coalition – www.globalwarming.org

Union of Concerned Scientists – www.ucsusa.org

United Nations Environment Programme – www.unep.org

United States Department of Energy– www.energy.gov

Washington Group International - www.wgint.com